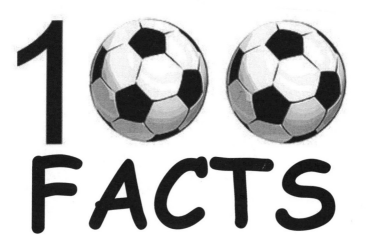

100
FACTS

ASTON VILLA

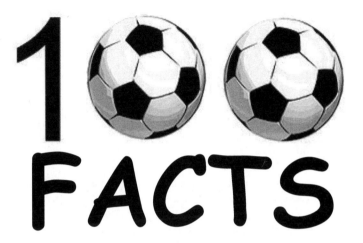

ASTON VILLA

Steve Horton

WYMER
WP
PUBLISHING
Bedford, England

First published in Great Britain in 2018
by Wymer Publishing
www.wymerpublishing.co.uk
Wymer Publishing is a trading name of Wymer (UK) Ltd

First edition. Copyright © 2018 Steve Horton / Wymer Publishing.

ISBN 978-1-908724-98-4

Edited by Jerry Bloom.

Typeset by The Andys.
Printed and bound by CMP, Poole, Dorset

A catalogue record for this book is available from the British Library.

Cover design by The Andys.
Sketches by Becky Welton. © 2014.

1874
VILLA CROSS
WESLEYAN CHAPEL

Aston Villa Football Club was formed by cricketers from the Villa Cross Wesleyan Chapel who were looking for a sport to play in the winter.

There are no definitive written records but folklore has it that four club members - Jack Hughes, Frederick Matthews, Walter Price and

William Scattergood - met under a gaslight in Heathfield Road in the Birchfield district of Birmingham. They were inspired by a game of football that was going on at a nearby field and decided that was the game they would play.

Price was nominated as the captain and Walter Midgley brought in as secretary. Within two weeks there were fifteen paying members but for that first winter no fixtures were organised.

Villa's first match did not take place until March 1875 and was against Aston Brook St Mary's at Wilson Road. They were a rugby club so the first half was played under rugby rules and the second half as association. Both sides fielded fifteen players and after a scoreless first half, Jack Hughes scored the only goal of the game in the second to give Villa a 1-0 victory.

1876
A CAPTAIN
AND A GROUND

Early in 1876 a twenty-one-year-old Scot saw Villa playing a practice match and asked for game. By the end of the year he was the club's captain and had arranged a ground for them.

George Ramsay was working in Birmingham as a clerk in a brass foundry. One day he was walking through Aston Park when he saw Villa's players practising and asked if he could take part. It soon became apparent that he had a lot of skill and knowledge and he was invited to join the club.

It wasn't long before Ramsay was put in charge of training and became captain. As a Scot, he had experience of the passing game and introduced it at Villa. This was a big difference to the usual English tactic of dribbling, rushing players or kicking the ball as far up field as possible.

Ramsay was instrumental in arranging the lease of a field off Wellington Road in Perry Barr. Players at first had to change in a blacksmith's shed, but the ground was enclosed and allowed the club to charge admission to spectators.

In 1884 Ramsay was appointed club secretary meaning he could quit working at the foundry. As secretary he was responsible for the arranging of fixtures, player recruitment, transfers and contracts.

1878
ARRIVAL OF
ARCHIE HUNTER

One of Aston Villa's great players in the Victorian era was Archie Hunter who was persuaded to join the club in 1878 thanks to the presence of George Ramsay.

Eighteen-year-old Hunter was playing for Ayr Thistle in Scotland and had reservations about moving to Villa. However his mind was swayed when he learnt that they were captained by Ramsay who was a fellow Glaswegian.

Hunter was said to be the 'prince of dribblers'. He had a reputation for being able to get the ball on the wing and dribble it until he crossed the goal line. He was one of the first household names in English football and only missed out on playing for Scotland as their FA refused to call up players who were based south of the border.

In 1887 Hunter became the first player to score in every round as Aston Villa triumphed in the FA Cup. In total he played 42 cup games for Villa, scoring 34 goals. After the Football League was formed in 1888, he scored nine goals in 32 appearances.

Tragedy struck in 1890 when Hunter suffered a heart attack and collapsed in a game against Everton. He never played football again and four years later he died at the age of 35.

1879
THE FIRST
SECOND CITY DERBY

The first meeting between Aston Villa and
Birmingham City, now known as the Second City
Derby, took place on 27th September 1879.

Villa's great rivals were formed in 1875
under the name of Small Heath Alliance,
referring to an alliance of cricketers from local
churches. In 1877 they moved to a ground in
Muntz Street, which would be their home for
thirty years.

Muntz Street was the venue for the first
meeting between the two clubs. It was a friendly
played on a Saturday afternoon and reports
suggested that Villa's players weren't impressed
with the state of the pitch, some saying it was
only fit for potholing. Villa lost the game 1-0, with
the goal being hotly disputed.

It was not until 1887-88 that the clubs
met in a competitive fixture, Villa winning an FA
Cup tie 4-0. By now their rivals were known simply
as Small Heath and they met each other for the
first time in the Football League in 1894-95, Villa
winning 2-1 at Wellington Road.

Small Heath became Birmingham in 1905
and City was added after World War Two. The
derby is now one of the most fiercely contested
in the country.

1879
FIRST
FA CUP MATCH

FACT 5

The first time Villa played in the FA Cup was in 1879-80, when their opening opponents were Stafford Road.

Villa received a bye in the first round before being drawn away to Stafford Road, a Wolverhampton based railway works side. On 13th December, Villa did well to secure a 1-1 draw against the beaten finalists in the previous season's Staffordshire Senior Cup.

The replay did not take place until 24th January 1880 and attracted a crowd of 2,000 to Wellington Road. Villa led 1-0 at halftime thanks to a goal from William Mason, who added another soon after the restart. Laws made it 3-0 after an hour and Stafford Road pulled one back shortly before the end for the game to finish 3-1.

In the third round Villa were drawn away to Oxford University, who had played in three previous finals. However the board decided to forfeit the tie rather than pay travel expenses for a game they were more than likely to lose.

The following season Villa progressed through three rounds of the FA Cup before being drawn against Stafford Road again. This time they weren't successful, the railway side winning 3-2 at Wellington Road.

1880
BIRMINGHAM
CHALLENGE CUP WINNERS

Villa won their first trophy in 1879-80 when they beat Saltney College in the final of the Birmingham Challenge Cup.

The final was played at Aston Lower Grounds on 3rd April in front of what the press described as "a capital crowd of 4,000 spectators". Davis put Villa ahead after half an hour but Saltney equalised soon before halftime.

After the break Villa had the advantage of playing with the wind and were soon in control of the game thanks to goals from Ramsay and Mason. They never looked like letting their lead slip and only excellent goalkeeping by Copley in the opposition goal prevented any further scoring.

Villa's victory made up for the disappointment of a week earlier, when they were beaten by Wednesbury Old Athletic in the final of the Staffordshire Senior Cup.

The following season Villa reached the final of the Birmingham Challenge Cup again, but were beaten by Walsall Town Swifts. They then won the trophy four years running. Now named the Birmingham Senior Cup, Villa's total of nineteen wins is more than any other side. However the last of these was in 1985 and they have not competed for a number of years.

The first Aston Villa players to be capped by England were Arthur Brown and Oliver Vaughton in 1882.

The Villa duo were selected to play for England in a friendly match against Ireland in Belfast on 18th February. Both made an instant impact in a game that saw England win by the huge score of 13-0. Centre forward Brown scored four while Vaughton, an inside left, hit five.

The following month both players were selected again, for two friendlies played in the same week against Scotland and then Wales. The first of these against Scotland in Glasgow saw Vaughton get on the scoresheet again, but England were hammered 5-1. They were beaten as well by Wales in Wrexham, by the score line of 5-3.

Brown never played for England again but Vaughton was selected for two British Championship matches in 1884. He was unable to add to his goals tally though as England lost 1-0 to Scotland then beat Wales 4-0.

Up until 2017 Villa had provided a total of 73 players for England. For many years this had been more than any other club, but in 2015 they were overtaken by Tottenham Hotspur.

1885
TURNING
PROFESSIONAL

FACT **8**

In 1885 Aston Villa became on of the first clubs
to pay their players after a new ruling by the
Football Association.

Up until then the game had been strictly
amateur but clubs were finding various ways
of getting around the rules, such as by paying
players to do other tasks required. Things came
to a head between clubs and the FA in 1884 when
Preston were expelled from the FA Cup following
a complaint by London side Upton Park.

Villa were one of a number of clubs
threatening to break away and form a rival
association, leading to the FA reaching a
compromise in July 1885. Players could be paid,
but only if they were born or had lived within six
miles of their ground for two years.

In their first season as a professional
club Villa had their worst FA Cup run since they
started entering the competition. After beating
Walsall Town 5-0 away from home in the first
round, they lost 2-0 at Derby County.

The summer of 1886 saw significant
organisational changes at the club, with George
Ramsay being appointed secretary after injury
forced him to stop playing. Success was now just
around the corner.

1886
CHOCOLATE
AND SKY BLUE

Aston Villa's traditional kit design originated
in 1886, although the shirts were chocolate
coloured rather than claret.

For the first twelve years Villa wore
various colours including black and white hoops
or stripes, green, black, and even white with red
spots, described as piebald.

In November 1886 press reports began
stating that Villa's players were wearing shirts
of chocolate and blue stripes as opposed to the
piebald design. In 1887 the chocolate became
claret and ever since then Villa's colours have
been claret and blue. Since 1893, they have
mainly been claret with blue sleeves and white
shorts.

The first claret and blue tops were woollen
and must have been unbearably hot at times.
They also had a drawstring collar and then a high
neckline from the 1920s. It was not until the
1950s that the club switched to cotton and the
crest was displayed on them.

Since the 1980s kit manufacturers have
had much greater influence on design and there
have been sponsors. For the inaugural Premier
League season in 1992-93 however, a retro kit
with drawstring was worn.

1887
THE FIRST
FA CUP TRIUMPH

FACT 10

Villa won the FA Cup for the first time in 1886-1887 when Archie Hunter scored in every round.

Villa thrashed Wednesbury Old Athletic 13-0 in the first round. They then beat Derby Midland 6-1 but needed three replays to finally overcome Wolves in the third round.

Further home wins for Villa over Horncastle and Darwen followed. In the semi-final they faced Glasgow Rangers, one of five

Scottish sides allowed in the competition. Villa triumphed 3-1 at Crewe to set up a derby final with neighbours West Bromwich Albion.

The final was played at Kennington Oval in London. Albion, beaten finalists a year earlier were slight favourites. It was estimated that about 8,000 of the 15,534 crowd had travelled down from Birmingham.

The Villa players were nervous early on but as the half progressed they got better and the score remained 0-0 at halftime. On the hour Villa took the lead with a classic breakaway goal. The ball was cleared to Hunter, who set up Hodgetts to score. With two minutes remaining Hunter seized on a poor back pass to poke the ball into an empty net to seal victory for Villa.

Hunter's goal in the final took his tally to eleven and meant he had become the first player to score in every round of the competition.

1888
FOOTBALL
LEAGUE FOUNDERS

Aston Villa was very much the driving force behind the formation of the Football League.

In March of that year Villa director William McGregor wrote to a number of other clubs suggesting the creation of a league competition. This would enable teams to have a guaranteed income stream instead of the unreliability of cup and friendly fixtures.

On 17th April the Football League was founded at a meeting in the Royal Hotel in Manchester, with McGregor its first chairman. Comprising of twelve clubs, teams would play each other twice a season. Initially it was proposed to award one point for a win and nothing for a draw or defeat, but eventually two points for a win and one for a draw was settled on.

The first round of fixtures took place on 8th September, with Villa's opening game away to Wolves ending in a 1-1 draw. The following week they beat Stoke 5-1 in front of 4,000 fans at Wellington Road.

Villa finished the season in second place, although they were eleven points behind runaway leaders Preston who were unbeaten all season. Their 9-1 win over Notts County was the biggest win by any side that season and their leading scorer was Albert Allen, who scored seventeen goals in 21 matches.

1892
RECORD
LEAGUE WIN

FACT **12**

Aston Villa's record league victory was on 12th March 1892, when they thrashed Accrington 12-2 in a game that saw three players score hat-tricks.

On a crispy cold but clear day described as perfect for football by the Lancashire Evening Post, Denny Hodgetts put Villa ahead in the first minute. Villa continued to dominate and had a number of shots saved before John Devey made it 2-0 and almost from the restart Johnny Campbell added a third.

Shortly before halftime two goals in quick succession from Devey completed a hat-trick

and put Villa 5-0 up at the break. Billy Dickson's shot for the sixth goal was so fierce it almost broke the net; soon afterwards Irvine scored for Accrington.

Campbell got the seventh and eight goals, which were both set up from crosses by Charlie Athersmith. Villa continued to dominate and Hay in the Accrington goal was the busiest player. When Hodgett's had to go off temporarily with an injury, Accrington took advantage and Thompson pulled one back to make it 8-2.

Villa responded swiftly to Accrington's goal and added four more before the end. Both Campbell and Devey scored to take their tally to four goals each, while Dickson got the other two to become the third player in the game to score a hat-trick.

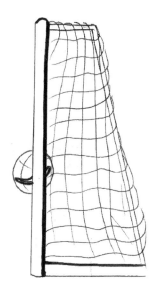

1892
THE FIRST
13 GOAL NET CUP FINAL

Aston Villa's second appearance in the FA Cup final was in 1891-92, the first time goal nets were used in the showpiece event. They again faced West Bromwich Albion, but could not repeat their victory of five years earlier.

Villa defeated Heanor, Darwen and Wolves to reach the semi-final where they were paired with Sunderland. At Bramall Lane in Sheffield, Villa went a goal down but come back to comfortably win 4-1.

The final with Albion on 19th March was again

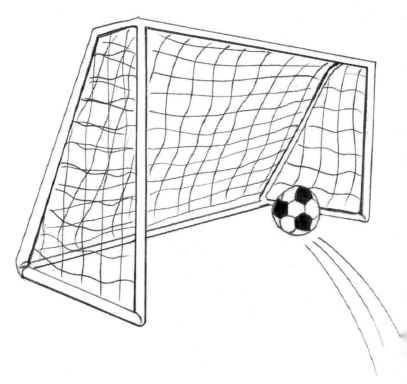

played at Kennington Oval and for the first time in a final the goals had nets. They had been patented in 1889 by Liverpudlian engineer John Brodie. Villa prepared for the big game by spending a few days in Holt Fleet by the River Severn then travelled to London the day before. Albion, in contrast, only left the West Midlands on the morning of the game.

The crowd of 32,810 was double that of 1887. As opposed to the last time the sides met in the final, Villa were favourites this time around but they found themselves 2-0 down within half an hour. A third Albion goal ten minutes after the break ended their hopes of a second cup victory.

1894
THE FIRST
14 LEAGUE CHAMPIONSHIP

Aston Villa won their first Football League Championship in 1893-94, having topped the table for most of the season.

A 3-1 victory for Villa in their fifth game of the season over Everton took Villa to the top of the league and they remained there. Villa were trained by the newly appointed Joe Grierson who placed an emphasis on strength and made players practice weightlifting.

At Wellington Road Villa lost just once, their form attracting crowds of up to 20,000. During the course of the season Villa beat every other side at least once with the exception of Wolves.

Only Sunderland looked like challenging Villa for the title but in the crucial games between the sides Villa won 2-1 at home and drew 1-1 away. They scored 84 goals in thirty games, the leading scorer being John Devey with twenty.

The title was secured in their last away game on 7th April, when Villa won 6-3 at Burnley, giving them a four-point lead over Sunderland with one game to play.

The following week heavy rain kept the attendance at the last game of the season at home to Nottingham Forest to 5,000. The local press described the players as being "enthusiastically received" and after trailing 1-0 at halftime Villa came back to win 3-1.

1895
WINNING THEN
LOSING THE FA CUP

FACT **15**

Aston Villa won their second FA Cup in 1894-95, only to have the trophy stolen from a local shop window.

Villa defeated Derby, Newcastle and Nottingham Forest on the way to the semi-final. Like in 1892 they were drawn against Sunderland, this time beating them 2-1 at Blackburn.

The final on 20th April was the first to be played at Crystal Palace and Villa's opponents were again West Bromwich Albion. Many of the 42,560 crowd were still

taking their positions when Bob Chatt scored for Villa after just thirty seconds. This remained the fastest cup final goal until 2009.

Villa found themselves under pressure for the rest of the first half but their defence held firm. After the break Albion seemed to run out of ideas and Villa had chances to extend their lead. There was no further scoring though and Chatt's early strike turned out to be the decisive goal.

The cup was loaned to football outfitter W. Shilcock so it could be displayed in his shop in Newton Row. However on the morning of 11th September it was discovered to have been stolen. Despite a £10 reward being offered it was never recovered and a new trophy was made by former Villa player Howard Vaughton, who had gone into business as a silversmith.

1896
"A PRIZE ALMOST AS GREAT"

FACT **16**

Aston Villa won the Football League Championship for the second time in 1895-96 thanks largely to their excellent home form. However it was deemed to be not so great an achievement as winning the FA Cup the previous year.

Villa were almost invincible at Villa Park, winning fourteen and drawing one of their fifteen games there. The biggest win was a 7-3 triumph over local rivals Small Heath, while they also hit five goals against Burnley and Stoke.

Villa's defence of the FA Cup was ended at the first hurdle when they lost 2-0 at Derby, who were also vying for the league title. However after the cup game Derby's league form stuttered and they fell off the pace. Villa remained remarkable consistency all season, only once going two games without a win.

On Friday 3rd April Villa won 2-0 at Nottingham Forest, meaning just one more point was needed from their final game to win the title. The following day as Villa entertained Hibernian in a friendly, closest challengers Derby could only draw at Burnley, confirming Villa as champions.

Despite the achievement of winning the league, the *Morning Post* did not feel it was the most prestigious trophy. Two days later the paper said that Villa had lost possession of the cup, but "secured a prize almost as great".

1897
WINNING THE LEAGUE
AND CUP ON SAME DAY

When Aston Villa won the Double of Football League Championship and FA Cup in 1896-97 they were confirmed as winners of both competitions on the same day.

After a slow start Villa went top of the league at the end of November. From the middle of January they were unstoppable and didn't lose another league game all season to establish a healthy lead at the top. They also reached the FA Cup final at Crystal Palace by beating Newcastle, Notts County, Preston and Liverpool.

The final was one of the most exciting in the competition's history. In front of 65,891 fans John Campbell gave Villa the lead with a 25-yard strike in the eighteenth minute but Everton hit back to lead 2-1 before half an hour had been played. Fred Wheldon brought Villa level and then a minute before halftime Jimmy Crabtree's header gave them the lead.

There were no further goals in the second half as Villa held on for victory. Afterwards there were further celebrations when they learnt that Derby had lost to Bury. This meant that Villa were confirmed as league champions with three games still to play.

Although The Double has been achieved on a number of occasions since, no team has claimed both trophies on the same day as Villa did.

1897
ASTON
LOWER GROUNDS

18

Aston Villa moved to the Aston Lower Grounds, which would later become Villa Park, in 1897.

The decision to move from Wellington Road was made in January 1896 and the club became a limited company to enable the raising of funds. Villa had played some games at the Aston Lower Grounds back in 1875 and were now keen to return to what had become a run down amusement park.

The development was overseen by chairman Fred Rinder with the help of architect E. B. Holmes. A former restaurant became the club offices, an aquarium became the gym and the groundsman took up residence in the rifle range.

A 5,500 seat main stand was constructed along Witton Lane and the other three sides were raised banking. A cycle track was also constructed to bring in extra revenue. The first game took place on 17th April 1897 when 15,000 fans saw Villa beat Blackburn 3-0. Two days later there were more than twice as many for a general sports meeting which included a match against Wolves, that Villa won 5-0.

The following year the ground was renamed Villa Park and before the end of the century had hosted its first international. In 1901, the first of what would be a record 55 FA Cup semi-finals was played there.

FACT 19 THREE MONTHS TO COMPLETE LEAGUE GAME

Aston Villa were involved in a situation that has never happened before or since when the final ten minutes of a league game were played more than three months after it had been stopped.

When Villa faced Sheffield Wednesday away from home on 26th November 1898 the kick off was delayed by the late arrival of the referee. This led to the game being abandoned due to bad light with ten minutes remaining and Villa trailing 3-1.

Football League officials said that the additional ten minutes would need to be played at a later date. At first Villa asked for those minutes to be played at Villa Park before the two sides met in the return fixture. This offer was refused and Villa were told they would have to travel back to Sheffield to complete the fixture.

To make the journey more worthwhile, Villa agreed to play a benefit match for one of the Wednesday players, in which the first ten minutes would constitute the missing minutes of the league game. This took place on 13th March 1899, with Villa conceding in those ten minutes meaning the result of a game started three months earlier was a 4-1 defeat.

1899
A CLOSE
FACT 20   TITLE FINISH

Villa won the Football League Championship in 1898-99 after one of the most thrilling finishes to any top flight season.

Villa went top of the table at the end of October and stayed there. At Villa Park they were unstoppable, remaining unbeaten there all season and drawing just twice. Away from home though they struggled however, winning four and losing eight of their seventeen games.

For most of the season Everton and Burnley were the closest challengers, but in April four straight wins by Liverpool brought the Merseyside club level on points. In a dramatic twist, the two sides were due to clash in the final game of the season on 29th April at Villa Park.

Villa had the better goal average meaning a draw would be enough to secure the title. However they put the matter beyond doubt before halftime, scoring five times without reply in front of over 41,000 spectators. Jack Devey got the first two goals and the others came from Billy Garraty, Jimmy Crabtree and Fred Wheldon

During the break a band played 'Au Revoir' (French for 'Goodbye'), much to the amusement of the home crowd. There was no further scoring in the second half and Villa were crowned champions for the fourth time that decade.

1900
NERVOUS WAIT
TO RETAIN TITLE

When Aston Villa retained the Football League Championship for the first time in 1899-1900 they faced a nervous wait. This was due to closest challengers Sheffield United still having games left after Villa had completed their fixtures.

Villa opened the season with two straight wins, the second of these being a 9-0 thrashing of Glossop at Villa Park. Despite this they were playing catch up for much of the season and by Christmas they were six points behind leaders Sheffield United. However a run of one defeat in their last thirteen matches took them to the top of the table.

Villa completed their fixtures on 16th April when they won 1-0 at Wolves. This left them four points clear of the Blades, who still had two games to play and had an inferior goal average. United were at Wolves themselves the very next day, but could only win 2-1 leaving them with an uphill task.

On 23rd April United travelled to Burnley knowing they needed an 8-0 win to get the title. They couldn't even managed a single goal, Burnley instead winning 1-0 meaning that Villa were champions by a two point margin, just as they were a year earlier.

1901
SHERIFF OF LONDON
CHARITY SHIELD

At the turn of the 20th Century Aston Villa contested the Sheriff of London Charity Shield on three occasions. However they were victorious just once in the showpiece match played between the country's top professional and amateur clubs.

Villa first took part in 1899, drawing 0-0 with Queens Park to share the six-foot high shield. In 1900 they lost 2-1 to Corinthian, who they faced again on 2nd March the following year at Crystal Palace.

Heavy rain on the morning of the game meant the pitch was extremely muddy but this didn't stop the game being played at a fast pace. Corinthian had the upper hand in the first half but Villa's defence was more than a match for their attack.

For the second half Charlie Athersmith was moved from outside right to a more central role and this soon paid off. Collecting a long clearance from defence, he raced clear of two Corinthian defenders before firing a shot past the keeper.

There was no further scoring and Villa's players were presented with the shield and medals by Mr Sheriff Lawrence. This was the last time Villa competed for the Sheriff of London Charity Shield, which came to an end in 1907 due to the dominance of professionalism.

1905
HARRY HAMPTON'S
CUP FINAL DOUBLE

Aston Villa won the FA Cup for the fourth time in 1904-05 with Harry Hampton scoring both goals in the final.

Villa were drawn at home in every round and beat Leicester Fosse, Bury and Fulham to reach the semi-final. After a 1-1 draw with Everton at Stoke, they won the replay 2-1 in Nottingham. This set up a final with Newcastle which was to be played at Crystal Palace.

Prior to the final Villa prepared at Rhyl in North Wales. 15th April was a glorious sunny day and 101,117 spectators were present at a game which was only two minutes in when Hampton opened the scoring. Collecting a pass from Bache, he beat the keeper with a low shot.

Newcastle rallied briefly and George made three good saves, but Villa were dominant for the rest of the half. Shortly before the break a massive scramble in the box saw Brawn hit the post, Bache the bar and Newcastle's keeper make a great diving save.

In the second half Newcastle had more of the play but they couldn't get past a stubborn Villa defence. With fifteen minutes remaining Hampton made it 2-0 when he reacted quickest to the rebound after Hall's shot was saved. Villa's greater experience had told and they were presented with their cup and medals by Lady Kinnaird.

1906
THE VILLA NEWS
AND RECORD

FACT
24

Aston Villa's match programme was published for the first time for the opening game of the 1906-07 season.

For Villa's match with Blackburn Rovers on 1st September, local journalist E. W. Cox was employed by the club to edit the publication, with 5,000 copies being printed by Colmore Press.

The programme cost one penny and featured plenty of news and articles. There was a photograph of captain Howard Spencer and a scoreboard from a cricket friendly Villa had played in the summer against Aston Unity.

As well as listing the fixtures for both Villa and Birmingham City's first and second teams, it also had information about forthcoming West Bromwich Albion and Wolves games. Fans arriving to buy the first copy though almost didn't have a match to watch. Blackburn's train was delayed but the game went ahead when they did arrive and Villa won 4-2.

The first Villa News and Record consisted of eighteen pages. A reprint was given out free with the programmes for a home game with Leeds in 1974 as the club celebrated their centenary, which many have come across and mistakenly thought they had an original. It has now grown into a glossy publication consisting of over seventy pages per issue.

1910
A RECORD SIXTH
LEAGUE TITLE

Aston Villa won a record sixth Football League Championship in 1909-10, the team's home form again being vital to the success.

Villa won seventeen and drew two of their nineteen home games. These included a 7-1 thrashing of Manchester United and they scored four goals on seven other occasions. Away from home they stayed consistent and the period from December to March was crucial to them, with Villa remaining unbeaten in fifteen league games.

The inevitable title was as good as secured with four games to spare. A 3-0 home victory over Preston on 9th April meant they were eight points clear but with a vastly superior goal average. They had the luxury of losing two of their last four games but still finished five points clear of second placed Liverpool. Their goal average was 2.000, far superior to Liverpool's 1.368.

This was Villa's sixth championship and then a record. It was their first for ten years, the all conquering team of the 1890s having grown old together. This latest title winning team was based on collective effort rather than individual brilliance. They failed to build on their triumph however and it would be 71 years before the club next won the championship.

1913
WORLD RECORD CROWD
26 SEES CUP WIN

Aston Villa won the FA Cup for the fifth time in 1913, beating Sunderland in the final in front of a world record crowd.

This was the first time that the top two teams in the First Division had contested the FA Cup final. Interest was immense and 121,919 descended on Crystal Palace. This was then a world record and apart from the 1923 final, the highest crowd for any football match in England.

Although Sunderland had won the league title Villa were the better side in the first half. They had a golden chance to score when a penalty was awarded after Clem Stephenson was fouled. However Charlie Wallace's kick was terrible and went several yards wide of the post.

In the second half Villa keeper Sam Hardy was injured and went off for ten minutes. Sunderland tried their best to take advantage of this situation and hit the woodwork twice. The game was rough at times, with Villa's Harry Hampton and Sunderland's Charlie Thomson clashing on a number of occasions.

With twelve minutes remaining Tommy Barber headed Villa into the lead. There was a huge scare towards the end when Sunderland hit the bar, but fans then had to endure an agonising seventeen minutes of injury time before the referee finally blew the whistle to confirm Villa's victory.

1914
RINDER & LEITCH'S
MASTERPLAN

In 1914 Aston Villa chairman Fred Ridner brought in famous football ground architect Archibald Leitch to develop Villa Park into one of the biggest stadiums in the world.

Villa's average crowd was less than 30,000 but Rinder unveiled a masterplan that would see Villa Park expanded to a capacity of 104,000. Shareholders would not agree to immediate wholesale changes, but were prepared to see a gradual redevelopment.

In the summer of 1914 the cycle track was removed and the terraces at either end squared up so they were closer to the pitch. The outbreak of war delayed the development of the new stand on the Trinity Road side of the ground and this was eventually completed in 1924.

In 1939 work began on extending the Holte End and this continued despite the outbreak of war again. This raised the capacity to over 75,000 and was as far as the masterplan was developed. Plans to have a terrace of a similar scale at the Witton End never came about, but Villa Park remained one of the England's leading grounds thanks to Rinder's vision.

1915
RECORD
LOW CROWD

The lowest ever crowd to watch Aston Villa in a home game was just 2,900 for a league fixture with Bradford City on 13th February 1915.

There were a number of factors behind the extremely low turn out. The most obvious was that since the outbreak of war at the start of the season many fans had joined the armed forces.

Bradford City were not the most attractive opposition and it was known that some players would be missing from each side. There had been snow in previous days but this was now being replaced by rain, meaning conditions on the terraces would be treacherous. To compound everything, Villa hadn't won any of their last five home games, which had included heavy 5-1 and 7-1 defeats.

Those who stayed away made the right choice. Chances were few and far between with Bradford happy to sit back and play for a point. Villa rarely broke through the resilient defence, having just one shot during the second half and also missing a golden opportunity when a player handled when about to shoot.

1918
KILLED IN
ACTION

The only Aston Villa player to be killed during World War One was Henry Dobson, who lost his life on the Western Front in 1918.

Dobson was nineteen years old when he joined Villa from non-league football in 1912. He was a hard working at both halfback and fullback but made only seven appearances over the next three seasons.

After joining the army reserve in December 1915 Dobson was called up into full service in February 1917. Whilst training that year he made a guest appearance for Rotherham County in regional competition.

Dobson was a member of the North Staffordshire Regiment fighting at St Quentin on 21st March 1918 when he was wounded during a retreat. He died from his injuries a week later and was buried at Premont Cemetery.

In 2017 Dobson was one of a number of footballers featured in a special film, *For Club and Country*, which was made for the National Football Museum in Manchester. Club Ambassador Ian Taylor was Villa's representative in the film, while commemorative trees were also planted in conjunction with the Woodland Trust.

1920
FIRST EXTRA TIME
CUP WINNERS

When Villa won what was then a record sixth FA Cup in 1919-20, they were the first to win the trophy in extra time.

Villa's opponents in the first post-war final were Huddersfield, who were looking to add a cup triumph to their promotion from the Second Division.

Four players who had appeared for Villa in the 1913 final were in the side this time around. There were 50,018 fans at Stamford Bridge, where Villa's centre half Frank Barson was warned by the referee about his tough tackling before the game had even kicked off.

On a warm day the game was not a classic. Both teams were well organised and cancelled each other out, with Villa just about enjoying the balance of play. The score was 0-0 after ninety minutes and with both sets of players tiring, if one team could score in extra time it would probably be enough to win the game.

In the game's 100th minute Billy Kirton's header, which took a deflection, gave Villa the lead. Their defence remained tight and held on to win the cup, which was presented to the players by Prince Henry, son of King George V. It was a record sixth FA Cup triumph, but it would be 37 years before they won it again.

1923
THE MURDER
OF TOMMY BALL

FACT **31**

The only professional footballer to be murdered whilst still playing was Aston Villa centre half Tommy Ball, who was shot dead by his landlord in 1923.

Ball joined Villa from Newcastle in 1920 but did not become a first team regular until the 1922-23 season. He and his wife rented a cottage in Brick Kiln Lane, Perry Barr, which was owned by George

Stagg who lived next door. The two men did not get on, with Stagg disliking the fact Ball kept chickens.

On 10th November Ball played for Villa in a 1-0 win at Notts County. This turned out to be the last of his 74 appearances for the club. The following evening he went to a local pub with his wife and on returning, went into the garden to fetch his dog only to be shot dead by Stagg.

Ball was buried in St John's churchyard and his grave has the inscription "To T.E. Ball – A token of esteem from his fellow players of Aston Villa F.C."

The following February Scragg was found guilty of murder and sentenced to death. This was commuted to life imprisonment and Stagg was subsequently declared insane. He eventually died in 1966 in a Birmingham mental hospital.

1924
ROYAL
VISIT

In 1924 a member of the Royal Family attended a match at Villa Park for the first time. The Duke of York, who later became King George VI, visited the league match with Bolton on 26th January.

The Duke was in the city to attend the annual dinner of the Birmingham Jewellers and Silversmiths Association. Three days beforehand it was confirmed that he would also be visiting Villa Park, having expressed a desire to attend the game.

A crowd of 56,000 were attracted by the royal visit and the Duke was presented to both teams before the kick-off. Len Capewell's first half strike was the only goal of a game in which both teams missed a lot of good chances.

Afterwards the Duke described the play as vigorous and said that it was the finest game he had ever seen. In 1936 he became King George VI, the father of Queen Elizabeth II.

In 2013 another future King, Prince William, visited Villa Park. The self confessed Villa fan took in a game with Sunderland that finished in a 0-0 draw.

33

1924
FIRST VISIT
TO WEMBLEY

Aston Villa's first visit to Wembley was in 1924 when they reached the FA Cup final, but they were unable to win the trophy for the seventh time.

Villa beat Ashington, Swansea, Leeds, West Bromwich Albion and Burnley on their way to the final, which was only the second to be played at Wembley. Their opponents were Newcastle United, whose only previous FA Cup win had been in 1907. To prepare for the big day, Villa's players spent two weeks training at Rhyl on the North Wales coast.

Rain had fallen heavily all morning and prior to kick off the touchlines had to be repainted due to being washed away. A brief period of sunshine was soon replaced by rain again after the game started. Many fans stood on the open terracing using their match programmes as umbrellas.

Villa had the better of the first half and Richard York was in good form. However they couldn't find a breakthrough, even when Newcastle's keeper Bill Bradley went off injured for several minutes after colliding with a post.

In the second half conditions got no better and players struggled to keep on their feet at times. To Villa's disappointment, two late goals meant the cup headed to the North East.

1926
GEORGE RAMSAY
LEAVES

FACT **34**

After an incredible 42 years in the role, George Ramsay finally retired as secretary manager in 1926.

Prior to his appointment in 1884, Ramsay had already been a pivotal figure as a player, captaining the side and helping secure the Wellington Road ground. However players were then amateurs and he also worked in a foundry, but as secretary manager he was full time.

Responsible for recruitment and contracts, Ramsay's extensive knowledge of the game saw him bring in the players that would go on to give the club great success. He was the linkman from the directors, who picked the team, to the trainer who got the players ready for matches.

Ramsay oversaw six League Championship and six FA Cup triumphs, putting him behind only Sir Alex Ferguson and Bob Paisley as English football's most successful managers. When he tendered his resignation he was 71 years old and Villa were one of the most prestigious clubs in the game. Even on his retirement, he remained involved with the club on an advisory basis and as vice-president.

When Ramsay died in 1935 he was buried at St Mary's Church in the Handsworth district of the city. His gravestone reads 'The founder of Aston Villa'.

1931
TOP FLIGHT
GOALS RECORD

Aston Villa hold the all time record for the most goals in a top flight season. However their tally of 128 in 1930-31 still wasn't enough to win the title.

The season opened with Villa beating Manchester United 4-3 at Old Trafford. They went on to score in each of their first 23 games, finally drawing a blank in a 2-0 defeat at Newcastle on New Year's Day.

Villa struck six or more goals on five occasions during the course of the season, which included an 8-1 thrashing of Middlesbrough, a 7-0 win over Manchester United and 6-1 wins both home and away against Huddersfield. Pongo Waring was their top scorer, netting 49 league goals.

Although they were formidable in attack, Villa's defence was leaky. They lost 6-4 at home to Derby, drew 5-5 at West Ham and were beaten 4-1 at Leicester. They conceded total of 78 goals over the course of the season, only three less than relegated Leeds.

Villa eventually finished the season in second place, seven points behind Arsenal. The champions scored 127 goals, just one less than Villa, but had a much better defence conceding only 59.

1931
BIGGEST WIN AT
ST ANDREWS

Aston Villa's biggest win at local rivals Birmingham City was 4-0 in 1930-31, the season they scored a record 128 league goals.

In the game, played on 21st February 1931 in front of a crowd of 55,000, Joe Tate scored an early goal for Villa. However the Blues were the better side for the rest of the first half and only poor finishing maintained Villa's lead at the interval.

After the restart the Blues continued their efforts to equalise but Jack Mandley scored to give Villa a 2-0 lead and deflate the home side. Villa took control after that, playing a swift passing game. They were especially dangerous down the flanks, taking advantage of the home side's influenza epidemic that led to three reserves being drafted in. Goals from Joe Beresford and Eric Houghton completed a resounding victory.

It was Villa's fourth successive win, a sequence in which they had scored 22 goals to keep up the pressure on leaders Arsenal.

Since 1931 Villa have beaten Blues at St Andrews on numerous occasions in the league, but only ever by one or two goal margins.

1933
TOP SCORER
RETIRES

The club's all time leading scorer is Billy Walker, who retired in 1933 after scoring 244 goals in 531 appearances.

Walker joined the club in 1915 but due to World War One had to wait until January 1920 to make his debut against QPR in the FA Cup. He scored both Villa's goals in a 2-0 victory and by the end of the season was in possession of a winners medal.

In October 1920 Walker made the first of eighteen England appearances. He captained both Villa and England, scoring double figures in twelve successive seasons. He got twelve hat-tricks during his time at Villa, one of them consisting only of penalty kicks.

Walker scored 214 league goals for Villa, one less than Harry Hampton. However he got two more goals than Hampton in the FA Cup to claim the record in all competitions. He was also Villa's record appearance holder until overtaken by Charlie Aitken in the 1970s.

At the age of 36 Walker retired from playing and took over as Sheffield Wednesday manager in December 1933. After World War Two he managed Nottingham Forest, leading them to FA Cup glory in 1959 after knocking Villa out in the semi-final.

1935
PONGO
WARING

One of Aston Villa's greatest ever strikers, Tom 'Pongo' Waring, left the club in 1935.

Waring was nicknamed 'Pongo' after a cartoon from the time and he had a reputation as a bit of a joker. He joined from Tranmere Rovers in February 1928. His first appearance in a Villa shirt was in the reserves and 23,000 turned out to see him score a hat-trick against Birmingham City.

Waring played thirteen times for the first team over the rest of the 1927-28 season, scoring seven times. The following season he was an ever present and got 32 goals.

In the record breaking 1930-31 season Waring scored 49 league goals. In all he found the net 167 times in 225 appearances for Villa and got a hat-trick on ten occasions.

Despite his excellent performances on the pitch Waring was terrible in training, with captain Billy Walker later recalling that he was often late and would sometimes drink unsold lemonade form the refreshment bars.

Waring was capped five times by England and there were protests when he was sold to Barnsley in November 1935. He later returned to Tranmere and remained living in Birkenhead. However when he died in 1980, his ashes were scattered at Villa Park in front of the Holte End.

1936
THE FIRST
RELEGATION

Aston Villa were relegated for the first time in their
history in 1935-36.

   The season started with Jimmy McMullan
having total control over team selection, the first
manager at Villa to do so. However he left in October
1935 and the board decided take over team affairs
themselves.

   Villa were in the bottom two for most of the
season. At home they suffered some particularly
bad defeats, conceding seven against Arsenal,
Middlesbrough and West Bromwich Albion. This was
the club's worst ever season defensively, conceding
110 goals.

   A win and two draws over Easter gave Villa
a glimmer of hope with two games left. Their fate
remained out of their hands though as although they
had climbed to fourth from bottom, teams below them
had games in hand.

   A 1-0 defeat to Arsenal left Villa on the brink.
They now needed to beat already relegated Blackburn in
their last match and hope other results went their way.
They were humiliated though, going 3-0 down inside the
first twenty minutes and eventually losing 4-2.

   The *Birmingham Daily Gazette* correspondent
placed the blame firmly on the directors, saying
the players were 'innocents in the piece'. Ironically
Blackburn, who would be joining Villa in the Second
Division were the only other founder members of
the Football League who had never previously been
relegated.

1938
SECOND DIVISION
CHAMPIONS

Promotion back to the top-flight came in 1937-38 as Villa were declared Second Division champions.

Under the guidance of manager Jimmy Hogan, Villa showed remarkable consistency all season. They never lost two games in a row and also didn't let a run to the FA Cup semi-finals distract their league form.

Promotion was all but secured in the penultimate game when Bradford City were beaten 2-0 at Villa Park. This left Villa four points clear of Manchester United and Coventry, who each had two games remaining but had a far inferior goal average. Three days later both those sides lost and Villa's promotion as champions was official.

The *Birmingham Daily Gazette* reported that Villa had "regained their proper status in the football world" while the board wrote a letter of thanks to all supporters that was published in the paper a few days later.

On 7th May 50,000 saw Villa comfortably beat Norwich 2-0 in their final game. As news was displayed that Birmingham had retained their First Division status, there were huge cheers from a crowd who could look forward to derbies again. At the end of the game there was a good-natured pitch invasion and later in the evening the team boarded a train to Southampton to begin a three-week tour of Germany.

Villa shared the Football League War Cup in 1944 as it was not possible to arrange a replay after the final was drawn.

With the Football League and FA Cup suspended due to the outbreak of World War Two in 1939, the War Cup was organised to try and maintain some national interest in the game. The competition was organised on regional lines with the north and south winners playing off for the trophy.

Villa beat Blackpool 5-4 on aggregate in the northern final, setting up a meeting with southern winners Charlton at Stamford Bridge on 20th May. The guest of honour at the match was the First Lord of the Admiralty and all proceeds went to the King's Fund for Sailors.

In front of a crowd of 40,000 Villa took the lead eleven minutes after halftime when Eric Houghton drove the ball through a crowded penalty area. Charlton drew level with fifteen minutes remaining through Charlie Revell whose shot gave Villa's keeper no chance.

The scores were level after ninety minutes and no extra time was played. With travel restrictions in place it was not practical to arrange a replay and each captain was presented with a miniature cup and the players received tokens.

The record home crowd was on 2nd March 1946 when 76,588 squeezed into Villa Park for an FA Cup game against Derby County.

World War Two had ended too late for the resumption of the Football League in 1945-46, but there was time to organise an FA Cup competition. For the only time in its history, ties were played over two legs.

Villa beat Coventry, Millwall and Chelsea to reach the quarterfinals, where they were drawn against Derby, with the first leg to take place at Villa Park. There was huge interesting the game, for which Villa's directors set aside 150 tickets for wounded servicemen.

The 76,588 spectators witnessed a thrilling game. Villa led three times only to concede twice in the last five minutes to lose 4-3, to the delight of Derby's 5,000 fans. In the second leg, Villa could only manage a 1-1 draw and went out 5-4 on aggregate.

The attendance for the game at Villa Park was 1,000 more than had been in the ground the previous time the record had been broken, against Manchester City in the sixth round in 1938. Derby went on to win the cup, beating Birmingham City in the semi-final and then Charlton Athletic at Wembley.

1947
OLDEST OUTFIELD
PLAYER

The oldest outfield player to represent Aston Villa was defender Ernie 'Mush' Callaghan, whose last game for them was at the age of 39 years and 257 days.

Callaghan joined Villa from non league football in 1930, having earlier been rejected by Birmingham City and West Bromwich Albion after trials. He was used sparingly and made just 125 league

appearances in seventeen years, although seven of these were interrupted by World War Two.

During the war Callaghan was a police constable in Birmingham and was awarded the British Empire Medal after rescuing trapped workers from a bombed factory. He also made some appearances for Villa and Solihull in regional competitions.

Callaghan remained on Villa's books when the Football League resumed in 1946-47, although it was as a reserve. On 8th April 1947 he stood in for the injured Vic Potts when Villa beat Sunderland 4-0 at Villa Park. This turned out to be his last game for the club and he later became head groundsman.

Callaghan remains Villa's oldest outfield player, although 59 years after his appearance the overall record was broken by keeper Brad Friedel. Callaghan died in 1972.

1950
A BRITISH
RECORD FEE

FACT **44**

When striker Trevor Ford joined Sunderland from Aston Villa in October 1950, it was for a British transfer record fee.

Villa paid £9,500 to Swansea for Ford, a Welsh international, in January 1947. George Edwards was moved from centre forward to right wing so that Ford could be accommodated. He repaid this faith by scoring nine goals in nine games in the second half of that season.

Ford was Villa's top scorer for the next three seasons. He was a no nonsense physical centre forward who was not afraid of shoulder charging defenders and goalkeepers. One of the highlights was when he scored four goals in a 5-1 win against Wolves on 27th December 1948.

By October 1950 Ford had scored 61 goals in 128 appearances. Sunderland — then known as the Bank of England Club, made a £30,000 bid which was accepted by Villa. Ford was bought a house by his new club and the following day he was dubbed the "world's most costliest player" by the *Daily Mail*.

Ford scored a hat-trick on his Sunderland debut and his scoring rate was similar to when he was at Villa. However there were tensions between him and strike partner Len Shackleton, a previous record transfer and he was sold to Cardiff for £30,000 in 1953.

1954
A RELUCTANT TRANSFER

FACT **45**

The club reluctantly agreed to let their best player Danny Blanchflower leave the club in 1954 after he submitted a transfer request.

Villa paid Barnsley £15,000 for the Northern Irish international right half in March 1951. He made his debut in a 3-2 win over Burnley at Villa Park, the *Birmingham Daily Gazette* naming him as man of the match for his excellent passing and setting up of attacks. His signing was a big boost to the side that only lost one of their last twelve games to avoid relegation.

For three seasons Blanchflower was a key player of the Villa side, showing a great ability to read the game. After falling out over training methods, he submitted a transfer request at the beginning of October 1954. Despite intensive efforts by the board to make him change his mind, he refused to do so and after three weeks it was reluctantly granted.

Blanchflower told reporters he hoped to move to London and on 8th December he joined Tottenham Hotspur for a fee reported to be £30,000. This was a British record for a midfielder. He had scored ten times in 148 league appearances for Villa and would have great success with Spurs, captaining them to the Double in 1961.

1957
THE SEVENTH
FA CUP

In the 1956-57 season Villa won their first trophy for 37 years when they won the FA Cup for what was then a record seventh time.

On their way to Wembley Villa beat local rivals West Bromwich Albion in the semi-final, winning 1-0 at St Andrews after a 2-2 draw at Molineux. First Division champions Manchester United were hot favourites to win the final with some bookmakers ranking Villa as 3/1 outsiders.

Early in the game Villa forward Peter McParland collided with United keeper Ray Wood, breaking the opposition player's cheekbone. Wood went off for treatment and returned as an outfield player, with Jackie Blanchflower going in goal.

After a goalless first half McParland scored with a diving header on 68 minutes. Six minutes later he doubled the lead, reacting quickest to score from the rebound after a shot had hit the bar. United pulled a goal back through Tommy Taylor with seven minutes remaining. Wood went back in goal to maximise their attacking threat but Villa held on for victory.

For several months afterwards, McParland was the subject of hate mail due to Wood's injury, even though his challenge on the keeper was fair. At the time it was a record seventh cup, but Villa haven't won the trophy since and four teams have overtaken their total.

1958
FIRST GAME WITH
FLOODLIGHTS

FACT **47**

The first full game to be played under floodlights at Villa Park was a friendly against Swedish side GAIS Gothenburg on 29th October 1958.

Earlier that decade many English sides had played prestigious friendlies against foreign opposition under lights, which were not allowed for Football League and FA Cup games. By 1956 the authorities were finally persuaded and two years later floodlights were installed at Villa Park at the cost of £35,000.

Villa's lights were first used for the latter stages of a league game against Portsmouth at the end of August. The first friendly against continental opposition was a low-key affair and attracted a crowd of 25,000. However with Villa struggling in the league those present were pleased to see them cruise to a 3-0 victory over a Swedish side that offered very little.

The following month another friendly was arranged against Scottish champions Heart of Midlothian. The attendance was again 25,000 and this time it was a far more competitive game. Villa twice came from behind to lead 3-2, although Hearts equalised to force a 3-3 draw.

Relegation for just the second time in the club's
history occurred in 1959.

Villa were in trouble from the start of the
season, losing six games in succession in September.
The board lost their patience with manager Eric
Houghton in November, when they threw away a
three-goal lead to lose 6-3 at Leicester. With Villa
bottom of the table he left by mutual consent and
was replaced by Joe Mercer.

After the New Year, Villa rallied briefly,
winning three games in a row in March. However
they failed to win any of their last nine fixtures.

Relegation was confirmed in cruel fashion
in the last game of the season on 29th April. Villa
were in total control and led West Bromwich Albion
1-0 at The Hawthorns only to concede an equaliser
two minutes from time. This draw, coupled with
Manchester City's 3-1 win at home to Leicester
meant that Villa had been relegated by one point.

Manager Joe Mercer had been so confident
of victory that he left the ground five minutes
early to attend a banquet in honour of England
international Billy Wright. Stunned at the news, he
responded by saying that the Second Division was a
tough league but predicted Villa's stay there would
be brief.

1960
STRAIGHT BACK UP
AS CHAMPIONS

FACT
49

Joe Mercer's prediction about Aston Villa's stay in the Second Division being brief was correct. They finished the season as champions to return to the top flight.

Villa started the season magnificently, losing just one of their first sixteen games to be top of the table at the end of October. They lost 2-1 at Liverpool on 7th November but responded perfectly, hitting double figures the following week when Charlton were thrashed 11-1 at Villa Park.

From Christmas there was little doubt that Villa and Cardiff would secure the two promotion places. Villa also had hopes of FA Cup glory but were beaten 1-0 by Wolves in the semi-final on 26th March. Four days after this they completed an astonishing comeback against Liverpool at Villa Park, recovering from 4-0 down to draw 4-4.

On 9th April Villa came from a goal down to beat Bristol City 2-1 to confirm their return to the First Division. They then won two of their last four games to finish the season as champions, one point ahead of Cardiff and nine clear of third placed Liverpool.

In the 1960-61 season Aston Villa became the first winners of the new League Cup competition... but not until the following season!

The competition was developed as a way of generating extra revenue for clubs and also to make use of floodlights, which were now commonplace at grounds around the country. It was not universally welcomed however and five clubs declined to take part.

Villa beat Huddersfield, Preston, Plymouth, Wrexham and Burnley to reach the final. This was to be a two-legged affair, with the opponents being Second Division Rotherham United.

Due to fixture congestion the final was held back until the beginning of the 1961-62 season. In the first leg at Rotherham's Millmoor ground, Villa went down 2-0 leaving them much to do if they wanted to claim the trophy and £750 prize money.

The second leg on 5th September attracted a crowd of over 30,000. Goals in quick succession by Alan O'Neill and Harry Burrows midway through the second half forced extra-time. With eleven minutes remaining Peter McParland scored the all-important goal to complete the comeback and send the home crowd wild.

Just a week after their triumph Villa began their defence of the trophy with a 4-3 first round win at Bradford City. They were unable to retain it however, eventually going out 3-2 in the third round to Ipswich.

1963
LEAGUE CUP
FINAL DERBY

Aston Villa reached the League Cup final again in 1963 but they were denied the trophy by local rivals Birmingham City.

Villa were drawn at home in every round, beating Peterborough, Stoke, Preston and Norwich on their way to the semi-final. They beat Sunderland 3-1 at Roker Park then drew 0-0 in the return leg to set up a two-legged final with their city rivals.

In the first leg at St Andrews on 23rd May, Villa fell behind in the first half but were level at the break thanks to a goal by Bobby Thomson. In the second half however Blues scored twice leaving Villa, who had been favourites, with an uphill task in the return leg.

Four days later in front of just under 38,000 fans Villa were frustrated by a defensive Blues side who marked Thomson out of the game. In what the *Birmingham Mail* described as "a dreary spectacle" there were hardly any shots, with the Blues happy to clear the ball into touch at every opportunity.

Villa rarely looked like coming back like they had in the 1961 final. They were then faced with the frustration of seeing their rivals lift the cup inside Villa Park.

1964
JOE MERCER'S
FACT 52 FORCED RESIGNATION

Promising manager Joe Mercer suffered a bout of ill health in 1964 and was then forced to resign.

Mercer came to Villa in the 1958-59 season but was unable to save the club from relegation. However the board kept faith in him and he repaid this with an instant return to the First Division along with success in the League Cup.

By developing the foundations laid by Eric Houghton, Mercer built a promising young team that got the nickname 'Mercer's Minors'. He was the first Villa manager to have total control over team selection and transfers.

From 1962 onwards Mercer suffered health problems and he had a stroke in 1964. Despite recovering, a club statement made on 10th July said that he had agreed to leave by mutual consent. His assistant Dick Taylor, who had been in control of team affairs while he was ill, replaced him.

Mercer indicated that although he had not exactly set the Midlands on fire in recent months, results hadn't been a true reflection of the team's potential. The following year he became manager of Manchester City, with whom he would win the Football League Championship, FA Cup and European Cup Winners Cup. Villa though found themselves going in the opposite direction.

1967
INEVITABLE
RELEGATION

In their fifth successive season of struggle Aston Villa finally succumbed to relegation in 1966-67.

For four seasons running, between 1962-63 and 1965-66, Villa finished in the bottom eight. They failed to win any of their first four games of 1966-67 then had a disastrous end of September, losing 6-2 at home to Chelsea then 5-0 at Leicester.

In October Tony Hateley, Villa's leading scorer for the past three seasons, was sold to Chelsea for £100,000. The failure to adequately replace him went a long way to condemning Villa to the drop. From November onwards they failed to put two wins together in succession all season.

In their penultimate game on 6th May Villa were beaten 4-2 at home by Everton, condemning them to the drop along with Blackpool. There had been a resigned acceptance for some time by players, fans and the board of Villa's inevitable fate.

The *Birmingham Daily Post* reported that too many times during the season there was no collective or individual effort to counter any side that a raised their game. Three days later the board took decisive action by sacking manager Dick Taylor, chief scout Jimmy Easson and assistant trainer Johnny Dixon.

1968
DOUG
ELLIS

With Aston villa in dire financial straits in 1968, a man took control of the club who would be synonymous with it for the next four decades.

In 1968 Villa were suffering mounting debts and were bottom of the Second Division. Under pressure from fans, the board resigned and London based financier Pat Matthews took control of the club. He brought in Doug Ellis as chairman, a self-made millionaire through selling package holidays.

Despite the change in ownership Villa were relegated to the Third Division in 1970 but Ellis oversaw a return to the top flight, only to be replaced as chairman in 1975. He was then thrown off the board four years later but predicted he would be back. He returned in 1982 after the European Cup success.

Ellis was nicknamed 'Deadly Doug' by former player turned television pundit Jimmy Greaves, who felt he had a lack of patience with managers and sacked them too often.

In the mid 1990s Ellis diluted his shareholding to allow funds to be raised for the rebuilding of the Trinity Road stand and purchase of new players. He remained chairman and the club's largest shareholder until 2006, when he sold up to Randy Lerner aged 82.

Ellis was knighted in 2012 for his services to charity and he is now a life president of the club.

1969
YOUNGEST
PLAYER

Jimmy Brown was just 15 years and 349 days old when he made his Aston Villa debut away to Bolton on 17th September 1969.

Manager Tommy Docherty was known for giving youth a chance and selected the Scottish schoolboy international as Villa sought their first league win of the season in what was their ninth game.

Villa were already 1-0 down when Brown had a shot that skimmed the bar in the twentieth minute. They were losing 2-0 at the break but Brown then had a hand in the goal that got Villa back into the game shortly after the hour mark. He passed to Brian Godfrey, who squared for Bruce Rioch to score.

In the following day's *Birmingham Daily Post* the headline was "Brown Sparkles But Villa's Revival is Left Too Late". Although Villa remained in trouble at the bottom of the table, the paper said that they could be encouraged by his gritty display.

The following year Brown signed professional forms and was a member of Villa's FA Youth Cup winning side in 1972. He stayed with the club until 1975, scoring once in 87 appearances. He later played for Preston, Ethnikos, Hibernian, Portsmouth and Worcester.

1970
BEST SUPPORTED
TEAM RELEGATED

Aston Villa were relegated to the Third Division for the first time in 1969-70, despite having the Second Division's highest attendance.

Villa had a dreadful start to the season and didn't win until their eleventh game. They could never get any consistency going, failing to win two successive games until the end of the season and only winning once away. Manager Tommy Docherty was sacked in January and replaced by former captain Vic Crowe.

A 2-1 defeat at Blackpool on 28th March looked to have left Villa with an impossible task, but two days later they beat Birmingham 2-0 at St Andrews, their only away win of the season. With four games left, Villa were still bottom of the league, three points from safety with four games remaining.

Villa then drew with Oxford and lost at Leicester. They ended their season on 13th April with a 1-0 home win over Sheffield United, taking them out of the relegation zone on goal average. However the two teams below them each had a game left and the following evening Villa's fate was sealed when Charlton beat Bristol City.

Despite the season of struggle, there was hope for the future. Villa's average attendance was 27,345, the highest in the Second Division and chairman Doug Ellis confirmed they were now financially stable.

The feelgood factor returned to Aston Villa in 1970-71 when they reached the final of the League Cup.

Villa fell short in the promotion race, finishing fourth and seven points off second place. In the League Cup they started in the first round and defeated Notts County, Burnley, Northampton Town, Carlisle United and Bristol Rovers but Manchester United were expected to be too strong for them in the semi-final.

In the first leg at Old Trafford Andy Lochead gave Villa a shock lead before Brian Kidd levelled for United. Just two days before Christmas 1970, a crowd of 58,667 squeezed into Villa Park where Pat McMahon's header was the deciding goal in a 2-1 win that took Villa to Wembley.

Villa's opponents in the final were Tottenham and for the majority of the game Villa were better than the First Division side. Lochead had a shot cleared off the line and Chico Hamilton hit the post. However Villa tired two goals in the last twelve minutes by Martin Chivers shattered their dreams of glory.

After the final whistle Villa's players were given a huge ovation by their support. There was a real belief that there could soon be a return to the good times and the following season they were proved right.

1972
CHAMPIONS WITH
POINTS RECORD

When Villa were promoted as Third Division champions in 1971-72, they went up in style, setting a points record in the process.

Villa opened their campaign with a 3-1 home win over Plymouth. They went on to remain remarkably consistent throughout the season, winning 32 out of their 46 league games.

For the second season running Andy Lochead was the leading scorer, although this time around he struck 25 times, almost double the previous season's tally. Villa enjoyed some emphatic wins, including a 6-0 away triumph at Oldham.

On 12th February Villa beat closest challengers Bournemouth 2-1 in front of 48,110 at Villa Park to set what was then an attendance record for the division. Promotion was secured in the third from last game. 7,000 Villa fans travelled to Mansfield where a 1-1 draw confirmed their place in the Second Division the following season.

The championship trophy was presented at the last home game of the season by Football League president Len Shipman. Villa beat Chesterfield 1-0 in front of over 45,000 fans to take their points tally to 70, beating the previous record of 69 held by Hull City.

Villa had got themselves out of the doldrums, but chairman Doug Ellis reminded fans that they had no right to get back to the top flight, it still had to be earned.

1974
VIC CROWE
SACKED

Manager Vic Crowe was sacked in 1974 after failing to develop the side into one that was capable of promotion to the top flight.

As a player Crowe made 292 league appearances for Villa between 1952 and 1964, mainly at right half after the departure of Danny Blanchflower. He was captain of the side that were promoted in 1960 and won the League Cup the following year.

After finishing his playing days with Peterborough and in the United States, Crowe was appointed manager of Villa in January 1970. He was unable to prevent them sliding to the Third Division for the first time in their history but a positive approach returned with a run to the League Cup final in 1971.

In 1971-72 Crowe led Villa to the Third Division title, breaking a points record. Their first season back in the second tier was encouraging and saw them finish third, although this was eleven points behind second place QPR.

After a disappointing fourteenth place finish in 1973-74, when they were only seven points ahead of the relegation zone, Crowe was sacked. He was replaced by Ron Saunders, who had taken Norwich City to the First Division for the first time in their history two years earlier.

1975
NON TOP FLIGHT
LEAGUE CUP FINAL

When Villa won the League Cup for the second time in 1974-75, it was the only major final at Wembley between two clubs who weren't in the First Division.

Villa beat First Division Everton in the second round, winning a replay 3-0 at Goodison Park. They then played lower division Crewe, Hartlepool and Colchester to reach the semi-final.

In the last four Villa were drawn against Fourth Division Chester City who gave them a major scare. In the first leg at Sealand Road Chester twice came from behind to draw 2-2. A week later at Villa Park, Villa led 2-0 only for Chester to fight back and level the scores. Eventually the tie was settled by Brian Little's goal ten minutes from fulltime.

At Wembley Villa faced Ron Saunders' former club, fellow Second Division side Norwich. The game was settled in the 81st minute when Ray Graydon's penalty kick was saved onto the post but he followed up and scored the rebound.

The final was the first and last to date between two clubs from outside the top flight and at the end of the season both clubs were promoted to the First Division.

1975
RETURN TO
THE BIG TIME

Having secured the League Cup, after eight years
in the wilderness Aston Villa topped the 1974-75
season with a return to the First Division — Ron
Saunders leading them to promotion with a second
place finish.

Saunders did not make wholesale changes to
the side he inherited. However he did add Leighton
Phillips and Frank Carrodus in midfield, whose
tenacious approach was just what his meticulous
preparation and demand for hard work required.

Villa stuttered around Christmas but extra
impetus was added with the introduction of
youngsters Bobby McDonald and Keith Leonard.
After New Year, Villa would go on to lose just once
in their last eighteen games.

A 2-0 victory over leaders Manchester
United on 22nd February was their sixth game
without defeat and made players and fans alike
believe that promotion was possible. They had it
secured with two matches to spare, meaning the
last home game against Sunderland on 26th April
was played in a carnival atmosphere. In front
of 57,000 fans Villa won 2-0, seriously denting
Sunderland's own promotion chances.

Villa completed the season with a 4-1 win
at Norwich, who also went up by finishing in third
place. They had won their last eight games, scoring
26 goals and conceding just three.

1975
INTO
EUROPE

Villa's first venture into European competition was short lived whey were knocked out in the first round.

Villa's victory in the 1975 League Cup final meant they qualified for the following season's UEFA Cup. They were drawn against Belgians Royal Antwerp in the first round, the first leg taking place away from home.

The home side's opening goal was scored after 26 minutes by Jos Heylingen. Villa then fell apart and Karl Kodat struck an eleven-minute hat-trick to leave them 4-0 down at halftime. With thirteen minutes remaining Raymond Graydon pulled a goal back to give Villa a slight hope for the second leg.

Antwerp's first leg hero Kodat ended the tie as a contest midway through the first half at Villa Park. There was no further scoring and the Belgians went on to face Polish side Slask Wroclaw in the next round, losing 3-2 on aggregate.

Villa's next UEFA Cup campaign in 1977-78 lasted longer. They defeated Fenerbahce, Gornik Zabrze and Athletic Bilbao to set up a quarterfinal with Barcelona. In the first leg at Villa Park they trailed 2-0 only to force a draw after two late goals by Ken McNaught and John Deehan. At the Nou Camp Brian Little gave Villa the lead but the Catalan giants came back to win 2-1 and go through.

1976
ASTON VILLA'S RECORD
63 APPEARANCE HOLDER

Charlie Aitken, who made more appearances for
Aston Villa than any other player, left the club in
May 1976 after seventeen years of loyal service.

Scottish left back Aitken came to Villa for
a trial in 1959 and was taken on along with Wilson
Briggs, who played in the same position. Briggs
would play only twice for Villa but Aitken broke into
the side in 1961-62 and remained the first choice
left back for fourteen seasons.

Aitken remained with Villa despite their
relegation to the Second and then Third Divisions at
the end of that decade. His goals were rare and he
once went five seasons without scoring in the league,
but did get four in 1971-72 as Villa won the Third
Division title. He rarely made a bad tackle and stood
in as captain on numerous occasions.

Aitken's loyalty to Villa paid dividends when
he was a League Cup winner in 1975. However
the following season, Villa's first back in the top
flight since 1967, he found John Robson offering
competition for his place.

In the summer of 1976 after 659 games for
Villa he went to North America to play for New
York Cosmos. It is unlikely his appearance record
will ever be surpassed.

1977
TWO REPLAYS
64 TO DECIDE FINAL

The League Cup was won for the third time in 1976-77 by beating Everton in a final that required two replays.

The first game at Wembley on 12th March was a dull 0-0 draw. Four days later at Hillsborough in Sheffield, Villa went ahead early in the game when Everton's Roger Kenyon scored an own goal. However just as Villa looked set to celebrate victory Bob Latchford equalised in the last minute and there was no further scoring in extra time.

The second replay at Manchester United's Old Trafford didn't take place until four weeks later. It was confirmed that if necessary penalties would be used as a decider. Villa went behind to a Latchford goal but with nine minutes to go Chris Nicholl equalised with a stunning strike from forty yards.

Just ninety seconds after Nicholl's goal, Brian Little scored with a cross shot to put Villa ahead but soon after Mike Lyons equalised to force extra time. Penalties looked inevitable but with little over a minute remaining Gordon Smith's cross wrong footed Terry Darracott and Little was on hand to smash the ball into the net from six yards.

There was no time for Everton to look for an equaliser and after five hours of football spread over four weeks and four days, Villa finally had their hands on the cup.

1978
GARY
SHAW

Birmingham born teenager Gary Shaw broke into Aston Villa's first team in 1978 and made a huge impact before his career was curtailed by injury.

Shaw was just seventeen when he made his debut as a substitute at Bristol City on 26th August that year. He played only twice more that season but in 1979-80 an injury to Brian Little allowed him more opportunities. The following season he struck up a brilliant partnership with Peter Withe, scoring eighteen goals as Villa won the title. He was also named PFA young player of the year.

When Villa won the European Cup in 1982 Shaw was the only local player in the team. The following season, after Villa beat Barcelona in the Super Cup final, the injured Argentinean Diego Maradona requested Shaw's shirt.

Shaw suffered a serious setback in 1983-84, injuring his knee in a game against Nottingham Forest. This kept him out for a season and a half and from 1986 to 1988 he played only seventeen league games, scoring once.

Shaw left Villa in 1988 and went on to play in Denmark, Austria and the English lower divisions for Walsall and Shrewsbury. He still lives in the West Midlands and is often seen at Villa Park either as a fan or in a media capacity.

66
1981
RECORD BREAKING
CHAMPIONS

When Villa won the Football League Championship
for the first time in 71 years in 1980-81, they did
so by setting a joint record by using only fourteen
players all season.

Villa were not among the pre-season title
favourites. However what they lacked in individual
quality they gained in togetherness, fitness and
team spirit. Ron Sanders got them playing as a
coordinated unit who would run through brick walls
for each other and instilled a belief that they could
win every game.

Villa lost two of their first eighteen games
but still weren't taken seriously by most pundits.
However a 2-0 win over favourites Liverpool on 10th
January did finally make people take notice. By April
it was a two horse race between Villa and Ipswich
Town, who won 2-1 at Villa Park on 14th April to
take command. However they lost their next two
games allowing Villa to regain the initiative.

On the final day of the season Villa faced
Arsenal at Highbury, needing a point to clinch the
title. They trailed 2-0 at halftime while Ipswich led
1-0 at Middlesbrough. In the second half Ipswich
conceded twice meaning that Villa were champions,
leading to joyous scenes amongst players and
supporters.

Seven of Villa's squad were ever presents. In
using fourteen players, they had equalled a record
set by Liverpool in 1965-66.

1982
RON SAUNDERS
QUITS

With Aston Villa through to the quarterfinals of the European Cup, Ron Saunders sensationally quit as manager in February 1982 and took over at local rivals Birmingham City.

Villa suffered more with injuries and struggled to defend their title, winning only one of their first nine games. By the beginning of February they were in the bottom half of the table but had beaten Valur and Dynamo Berlin to reach the last eight of the European Cup.

On 9th February Saunders stunned the football world when he resigned over a contractual dispute, the full circumstances of which have never been fully disclosed. To try and maintain some stability, his assistant Tony Barton was promoted to the managerial role.

Within days there was a sensational development when Saunders was unveiled as the new manager of Birmingham City. Blues were battling relegation and in another strange twist of fate Saunders' first game in charge of his new club was against Villa. In that game at St Andrews, Peter Withe scored the only goal to give Villa a 1-0 victory.

Saunders remained at St Andrews for four years before taking over at West Bromwich Albion. He was dismissed from there in 1987 at the age of 55 and that turned out to be his last managerial role.

FACT 68

1982
CHAMPIONS OF
EUROPE

Villa overcame their poor league form and
managerial upheaval to win the European Cup in
1982, beating one of the continent's biggest names
in the final.

Villa knocked out Valur and Dynamo Berlin but
by the time of their quarterfinal tie with Dynamo
Kiev, Tony Barton had been appointed manager.
After a 0-0 draw in the USSR Villa won the return
2-0 at Villa Park. In the last four Tony Morley's
27th minute goal in the first leg at Villa Park was
enough to take them to the final.

Three times champions Bayern Munich were
overwhelming favourites in Rotterdam on 26th May.
Villa were dealt a huge blow in the tenth minute
when keeper Jimmy Rimmer injured his shoulder. He
was replaced by Nigel Spink, making just his second
appearance for the club.

Spink put in an inspired performance making a
number of saves to keep Bayern at bay, then in the
67th minute Peter Withe scored from close range
after being set up by Morley. Bayern thought they
had equalised with three minutes remaining, but the
goal was ruled out for offside and Villa held on for
victory.

On arrival back in Birmingham the cup was
filled with champagne and paraded through the
streets. The following season they defended their
title, but were eliminated in the quarterfinal by
Juventus.

1983
SUPER CUP
WINNERS

Aston Villa won the 1982 European Super Cup in a final that was not played until the following year.

The trophy contested by the winners of the European and European Cup Winners Cups was then played over two legs. Villa's opponents were Barcelona, who were going through something of a lean spell and hadn't won the Spanish league title since 1974.

Barcelona had Diego Maradona in their ranks, but he missed both games through illness. In the first leg on 19th January, the Nou Camp was less

than half full as Marcos Alonso scored the only goal of the game in the 52nd minute.

A week later the game remained goalless until ten minutes from the end when Gary Shaw swept the ball home from ten yards to force extra time. In the first period Gordon Cowans scored from the penalty spot after Mark Walters was fouled and Ken McNaught added another to give Villa a two-goal advantage.

There was no way back into the game for a bad tempered Barcelona side, who had been reduced to nine men thanks to two red cards. Every Villa pass was cheered and at the end Villa captain McNaught was presented with the cup, which was actually a piece of wood with the UEFA badge on it.

1985
DENNIS MORTIMER
LEAVES

Villa's European Cup winning captain left the club in 1985 after ten years at Villa Park.

Originally from Liverpool, Mortimer failed to be picked up by that city's two big clubs and went through the junior ranks at Coventry City. The midfielder was signed by Ron Saunders on Christmas Eve 1975 and starred in a 4-1 victory over West Ham on Boxing Day.

Mortimer developed into a key figure in the Villa side and by the time of the European Cup campaign was the longest serving player. He was a driving force who inspired others with his surging runs from midfield. Although capped by England at under-23 and B level he never made a full international appearance for his country.

The endearing image of Mortimer to Villa fans was undoubtedly him lifting the European Cup in Rotterdam. By the time he left for Brighton at the age of 33 he had made 403 appearances in all competitions, scoring 36 times.

After retiring from playing Mortimer was often a pundit for local radio at Villa matches. He has also coached at West Bromwich Albion and been on the after dinner speaking circuit.

1987
DOWN TO
THE SECOND DIVISION

Just five years after being crowned champions of Europe, Aston Villa were relegated to the Second Division after a dismal campaign in 1986-87.

When Tony Barton was sacked in 1984 he was replaced by Shrewsbury boss Graham Turner; a surprise appointment given that he had no First Division management experience. Villa finished in the top half in 1984-85, but the following season only three wins from their last five games saved them from the drop.

An opening day 3-0 defeat at home to Tottenham didn't bode well for 1986-87 and after five defeats in the opening six games Turner was sacked. His replacement was Billy McNeill, who started with a creditable 3-3 draw at champions Liverpool. Four wins in the next five games followed, but his bright start was ended with a defeat at his former club Manchester City.

The defeat at City was the start of a miserable sequence of just one win in twenty league games. With four games to go Villa were seven points adrift and relegation was confirmed in the penultimate game, a 2-1 home defeat to Sheffield Wednesday.

McNeil was sacked before the final game of the season, a 3-1 defeat at Manchester United. It meant they finished the season in bottom place with 36 points.

1988
SNEAKING
72 BACK UP

Aston Villa secured promotion back to the top flight in last gasp fashion in 1987-88, taking advantages of rivals' failings on the last day of the season.

The season got off to the worst possible start when Villa lost 2-0 to Birmingham City in their first home game. After winning just one of their opening six games new manager Graham Taylor's side finally gelled. A 0-0 home draw with Barnsley attracted only 12,641 fans but it was the start of an amazing run of just one defeat in 25 games.

Taylor's side had no stars, it was made of journeymen professionals who knew how to work hard to get out of the Second Division. Wins were sometimes ground out rather than gained in style. Leading scorers Gary Thompson and Warren Aspinall each netted just eleven goals.

After Villa went out of the FA Cup to Liverpool in the fourth round, league form faltered and they lost six out of their next ten games. This meant that on the last day of the season automatic promotion was out of their hands. However despite only managing a 0-0 draw at Swindon, rivals Middlesbrough and Bradford both lost at home meaning Villa were up on goal difference.

1988
LUCKY
THIRTEEN

Aston Villa met local rivals Birmingham City in two cup competitions in the early part of the 1988-89 season. They twice broke the record for the biggest winning margin in the fixture and had a total goals tally of 13-0.

The two sides were first drawn against each other in the two-legged second round of the League Cup. This was the first time they had met in the competition since the 1963 final that the Blues had won.

In the first leg at St Andrews on 27th September Villa won 2-0. Two week later they completed their progress to the next round with a comfortable 5-0 win. This was the first time either side had won this fixture by more than four goals.

Just four weeks later on 9th November Villa and the Blues faced each other again at Villa Park. This time the competition was the Full Members Cup; a short-lived trophy competed for by clubs in the top two divisions.

Even though it was a derby, the competition didn't capture the imagination of the public and there were just 8,324 fans inside the stadium. They witnessed a piece of Second City derby history though as Villa broke the record again. This time they thrashed Blues 6-0, a margin that has not been matched since.

In 1989 Aston Villa signed a player who had been encouraged to retire by his previous club but who defied the odds to become a key figure at Villa Park.

Irish international defender Paul McGrath had spent seven years at Manchester United but was having recurring knee problems. He was offered a retirement package and testimonial but refused this, leading to Villa manager Graham Taylor paying £400,000 for his services.

McGrath defied the medical professionals by continually putting in good performances after a special training regime was developed for him. He was twice a league runner up and won two League Cups with Villa. At the end of the 1992-93 season he was voted player of the year by his fellow professionals.

In seven seasons at Villa McGrath made 323 appearances in all competitions. After leaving he had brief spells at Derby County and Sheffield United, but retired from playing in November 1997.

Despite having left Villa more than twenty years ago he remains one of the club's greatest ever players in the eyes of the fans. His terrace chant 'Paul McGrath My Lord', to the tune of *Kumbaya*, continues to be sung today.

1990
TITLE
CHALLENGE

After only just avoiding relegation in 1988-89 Aston Villa pushed Liverpool all the way in the title race the following season, eventually finishing second.

On their return to the top flight Villa finished just one place and one point outside the relegation zone. They then lost leading scorer Alan McInally to Bayern Munich and no major new signings came in for the following season.

After winning only one of their first seven games manager Graham Taylor had the side playing as an organised unit who slowly but surely moved up the table. Between October and February they won fifteen out of eighteen games, taking them to within a point of Liverpool but with two games in hand.

Midfielder David Platt was a revelation, putting in performances that earned him an England call-up and being named player of the year by his fellow professionals. He was Villa's leading scorer with 24 goals, surpassing McNally's total of the following season.

Eventually Villa's inexperience caught up with them. They won only three of their last nine while Liverpool didn't lose any. Villa ended the season nine points behind the Reds but this had flattered the champions. Taylor's managerial skills had been noted by the FA too, who appointed him as England manager after that summer's World Cup.

76

1990
INTER
MILAN

One of the greatest European nights ever seen at Villa Park was on 24th October 1990 when the mighty Inter Milan were beaten 2-0 in the UEFA Cup.

In 1990-91 English clubs were allowed back in Europe for the first time since the ban imposed after the Heysel Stadium disaster of 1985. Villa qualified for the UEFA Cup courtesy of their second placed finish in the league, meaning they would be in Europe for the first time since 1982-83.

Villa defeated Banik Ostrava to set up the second round tie against the European giants, whose side contained three of the German squad that had won that summer's World Cup.

After fourteen minutes Villa took the lead through the most unlikeliest source. Danish defender Kent Nielsen's 25-yard piledriver gave Walter Zenga in the Inter goal no chance, sending the Holte End wild. Midway through the second half David Platt scored the second from close range after a good pass by Gordon Cowans. It could have been many more, with Zenga being in top form.

Two weeks later in the San Siro stadium Villa were 1-0 down after just seven minutes. They held on until halftime but two second half goals completed the Inter comeback. Four years later the sides were paired together again, with Villa going through on penalties.

1991
DR JOZEF
SACKED

Aston Villa were the first top flight English club to appoint a manager from outside the British Isles. However the reign of Jozef Venglos ended after just one season when he left in 1991.

After Graham Taylor left to take the England job Villa turned to Venglos, who had just guided Czechoslovakia to the World Cup quarterfinals. Fourteen years earlier his Czechoslovak side had won the European Championships and he had twice won the domestic title with Slovan Bratislava.

Chairman Doug Ellis claimed that Venglos was the best coach in Europe. A doctor of physical education, he spent a lot of time studying the technical aspects of the game and was also interested in philosophy.

Venglos arrived at a time when nutrition and individual fitness plans were unheard of in the English game. Players used to eating steaks and drinking as much alcohol as they liked, struggled to adapt to his strict regime.

Although Villa didn't start the season too badly, fortunes dipped after they went out of the UEFA Cup to Inter Milan, winning just two from their next eleven league games. After finishing the season in seventeenth place, Venglos resigned before Ellis had a chance to sack him.

1991
BIG RON
ATKINSON

After the departure of Jozef Venglos, Aston Villa returned to traditional methods and appointed an established English manager.

A former manager of West Bromwich Albion, Manchester United and Atletico Madrid, Ron Atkinson's appointment at Villa was a controversial one. He had just led Sheffield Wednesday to promotion and a League Cup triumph but then joined Villa a week after promising to stay in South Yorkshire.

By a strange twist of fate Atkinson's first game in charge of Villa was away to Wednesday. Villa won 3-2 and they went on to finish the season in a much-improved seventh place. The following season they pushed Manchester United all the way in the league, eventually finishing second.

In Atkinson's third season in charge Villa won the League Cup, their first trophy since they were European champions in 1982. However the squad was ageing and Atkinson's relationship with chairman Doug Ellis had been strained for two years.

In 1994-95 Villa struggled and won just two of their first fourteen games. Their side was ageing and in the relegation zone when Atkinson was sacked following a 4-3 defeat at Wimbledon. He was replaced by Brian Little, who guided the club to safety. Atkinson remains one of only two English managers, the other being Kevin Keegan, who have finished second in the Premier League.

FACT 79

1993
PREMIER LEAGUE
RUNNERS UP

In the inaugural season of the Premier League, Aston Villa finished as runners up to champions Manchester United.

For the 1992-93 season the old First Division became the Premier League. This was because clubs had broken away from the Football League to secure more television revenues.

There was little sign at the start of the season that Villa would be involved in a title challenge. They didn't win until their fifth game and in September the signing of Dean Saunders for a record £2.5 million was a catalyst for a climb up the table.

Saunders scored twice in his second game as Villa beat his former club Liverpool 4-2. This took them up to first place and by Christmas they were in a three-way battle for the title with United and surprise contenders Norwich City. Saunders was a persistent threat up front alongside Dalian Atkinson and Dwight Yorke.

On 14th March Villa secured a vital point at United but then lost at Norwich. A 3-0 defeat at Blackburn on 21st April was particularly damaging and then on 2nd May a surprise 1-0 home defeat to relegation threatened Oldham handed United the title.

Villa eventually finished ten points behind United and qualified for the UEFA Cup. They have not finished in as high a position since.

1994
LEAGUE CUP
WINNERS

Aston Villa upset the formbook in 1993-94 to win the League Cup for the fourth time, beating favourites Manchester United in the final.

Villa's road to the final saw them overcome local rivals Birmingham over two legs and require a penalty shootout to beat Tranmere Rovers in the semi-final. Treble chasing United were the opponents at Wembley, few pundits giving Villa much chance of success.

Manager Ron Atkinson played a five-man midfield that did a good job of stifling United's attack. Paul McGrath was outstanding in defence, totally snuffing out the threat of Eric Cantona. After 25 minutes Dalian Atkinson gave Villa the lead, scoring after receiving a beautiful flicked pass from Dean Saunders.

Twenty minutes into the second half United's Lee Sharpe looked certain to score but was denied by Kevin Richardson. Six minutes later Richardson set up Villa's second goal, taking the free kick that Saunders poked into the net.

Mark Hughes scored for United with seven minutes left and moments later his volley was well saved by Mark Bosnich. Rather than hold on in injury time Villa attacked and when Atkinson's goalbound shot was handled on the line by Andrei Kanchelskis, Saunders converted the penalty.

Villa went on to finish the season in tenth place; their Wembley victory denying United an unprecedented domestic treble.

1994
END OF THE
HOLTE END

Villa Park's famous Holte End terrace was demolished at the end of the 1993-94 and replaced with a new single tier stand.

Following the death of 96 Liverpool fans at the Hillsborough disaster of 1989, the government introduced legislation stating that all top flights grounds had to be all seated by the start of the 1994-95 season.

By then the Holte End, with a capacity of over 19,000 was the largest end terrace in England. Rather than just plonk seats onto the existing terrace, plans were drawn up for a two tier stand offering unobstructed views, the outside of which would have a traditional red-brick frontage.

On 7th May 1994 all 19,210 fans that stood on the Holte End for the last time as Villa faced Liverpool were given a sponsored certificate stating 'I was there'. After trailing 1-0 at halftime, Villa came back to win 2-1 with both goals coming from Dwight Yorke. There were celebrations at the end as players did a lap of honour with the League Cup.

Within hours of the final whistle the bulldozers had moved in. Progress on the new stand was extremely fast and by the end of the year all 13,462 seats of what was then the largest goal stand in England were installed.

1996
LEAGUE CUP
WINNERS

The League Cup was won for the second time in three years in 1995-96.

Villa beat Peterborough 7-1 on aggregate in the second round and then enjoyed home successes over Stockport, QPR and Wolves to take them to the semi-final. They overcame Arsenal on away goals to advance to Wembley where their opponents were Leeds United.

Savo Milosevic gave Villa the lead with a stunning dipping drive after twenty minutes. The Serb had not lived up to expectations since joining Villa the previous summer but this was just the type of goal that had persuaded Brian Little to sign him.

Villa continued to dominate the game and Leeds didn't start looking dangerous until just before halftime. Ten minutes into the second half Villa extended their lead when a poor clearance was seized upon by Ian Taylor to score.

Leeds rarely troubled Villa for the rest of the game and with a minute to go Milosevic broke free and passed to Dwight Yorke. The Trinidadian made no mistake, smashing it in off the underside of the crossbar to make it 3-0.

This was Villa's fifth League Cup, at the time equalling Liverpool's record. As of 2018, it remains the club's last major trophy.

Aston Villa's best run in Europe since the European Cup campaigns of the 1980s was in 1997-98 when they reached the quarterfinals of the UEFA Cup.

In the first round Villa were drawn against French side Bordeaux, finalists two years earlier. After a 0-0 draw in France, extra time was needed in the home leg for Villa to edge through 1-0. The second round saw Villa draw 0-0 in Spain against Athletic Bilbao in Spain, before they won 2-1 at home.

Steaua Bucharest were the third round opponents and Villa lost 2-1 in Romania before overturning the deficit at home, winning 2-0. In the quarterfinal Villa faced another Spanish side, Atletico Madrid. After Villa lost 1-0 in the Vicente Calderon stadium, Villa Park was packed to capacity on 17th March to see if they could overturn the deficit.

Jose Luis Caminero scored for Atletico in the twelfth minute. With eighteen minutes to go Ian Taylor scored with a deflected shot to give Villa a glimmer of hope. Two minutes later the stadium was bouncing when substitute Stan Collymore levelled the scores on aggregate with a stunning drive from the edge of the area.

Villa poured forward and Lee Hendrie forced a great save from the keeper but Atletico held on to go through on away goals.

1998
BEST START
TO A LEAGUE SEASON

Aston Villa's best start to a Premier League season was in 1998-99 when they were unbeaten for the first twelve games.

After Brian Little resigned in February 1998 with Villa fifteenth in the table former player John Gregory took over. He oversaw an improvement in form and they rose to seventh and UEFA Cup qualification.

Despite losing striker Dwight Yorke to Manchester United at the start of 1998-99 the signing of former Arsenal player Paul Merson for half the price was an inspirational one. After drawing 0-0 at Everton in their first game Villa won four in succession and topped the table by the middle of September.

At the beginning of November Dion Dublin arrived from Coventry and was an instant success, scoring twice in a 3-2 home win over Tottenham then getting a hat-trick as Villa won 4-1 at Southampton.

On 21st November Villa were three points clear at the top when Liverpool came to Villa Park. Dublin was again on target scoring twice but Villa went down 4-2, their first defeat coming in the thirteenth game.

Villa were still in first place at New Year but a run of seven defeats in eight games saw them drop to sixth. They rallied briefly in April with three straight wins but then lost their last three and failed to qualify for Europe.

1999
EUROPEAN FINAL
HOSTS

FACT **85**

Villa Park's status as a top class stadium was confirmed when it hosted the last European Cup Winners Cup final in 1998-99.

The stadium's superior spectator, players and media facilities, coupled with Birmingham's excellent transport links and hotel capacity, led to UEFA choosing Villa Park to host the 1999 final. There would be no English involvement however, with Chelsea being knocked out by RCD Mallorca in the semi-final.

The Spanish side's final opponents were Italy's Lazio, managed by future England boss Sven Goran Eriksson. This meant that there was guaranteed to be a first European trophy for one of the finalists.

Christian Vieri gave Lazio the lead after seven minutes but within four minutes Dani had equalised. Mallorca had much the better of the second half but it was Lazio who snatched victory with nine minutes remaining. Following a poor clearance by Mallorca's captain Javier Olaizola, Pavel Nedved curled a shot past Carlos Roa.

There was no way back for the Spaniards, whose fitness was far inferior to that of Lazio. Nedved was substituted to a huge ovation from fans as his side held on for victory. Lazio had won their first European trophy and were the last winners of the Cup Winners Cup, which the following season was merged into an expanded UEFA Cup.

Aston Villa were losing finalists in the last FA Cup final to take place at the old Wembley Stadium before it was demolished to make way for a new construction.

Villa were drawn at home in their first three ties, knocking out Darlington, Southampton and Leeds. They won 2-1 at Everton in the 6th round and were drawn against Bolton Wanderers in the semi-final. After a 0-0 draw at Wembley, Villa won 4-1 on penalties to reach the final where their opponents were Chelsea.

The first half was a dull affair and after the break Villa were more up against it as Chelsea attacked more. Dennis Wise had a goal disallowed for offside and George Weah missed several chances. Villa's best opportunity fell to Gareth Southgate but he headed wide.

There were seventeen minutes remaining when Chelsea were awarded a free kick that was taken by Gianfranco Zola Villa keeper David James came to collect it but dropped the ball and it rebounded off Southgate into the path of Roberto Di Matteo, who fired it into the roof of the net.

Villa's best chance to equalise fell to Benito Carbone but his shot was straight at keeper Ed de Goey. The next six finals were played in Cardiff while Wembley was built, but Villa failed to reach any of them.

2001
INTERTOTO CUP
WINNERS

FACT **87**

Aston Villa qualified for the UEFA Cup in 2001 by being one of three winners of UEFA's summer competition, the Intertoto Cup.

Villa joined the tournament at the third round stage in July, coming back from a 2-1 first leg deficit to beat Croats Slaven Belupo 3-2 on aggregate.

In the next round they lost the first leg 2-1 away to French side Rennes, a last minute goal from Darius Vassell giving them a lifeline. Dion Dublin's fifth minute goal in the return leg was enough to take them through on away goals.

Villa were now in one of three finals and faced Swiss side Basel. Paul Merson scored Villa's goal in

the first leg as the two sides drew 1-1 at St Jakob Park. In the return there was a capacity crowd to see Australian Scott Chipperfield give Basel a first half lead. Vassell equalised on the stroke of halftime and in the second half two goals from Juan Pablo Angel and one from David Ginola saw Villa cruise to victory.

Villa took their place in the UEFA Cup alongside other winners Paris Saint Germain and Troyes. However their European adventure didn't last much longer and they were knocked out in the first round by Croat side Varteks.

2006
RANDY
LERNER

With his health failing, Doug Ellis relinquished his control of Aston Villa in 2006 with American businessman Randy Lerner taking over the ownership of the club.

Lerner was the owner of NFL franchise side Cleveland Browns and claimed to have taken an interest in Villa whilst a student at Cambridge University in the 1980s. In gaining control of Villa, he became just the second American to own an English Premier League club. Lerner appointed himself as chairman and made Ellis, whose association with the club went back to 1968, a life president.

Lerner's ownership of Villa lasted ten years and saw a number of managers come and go after Martin O'Neill resigned in 2010. Criticism was directed at him after the departure of O'Neill and sale of the club's best players.

In 2014 the club was put up for sale with an asking price of £200 million. However it was not until May 2016 and Villa's relegation to the Championship that they were finally sold. Chinese businessman Tony Xia's Recon Group took control for the knocked down price of £76 million.

2008
BIG DERBY
WIN

On 20th April 2008 Villa beat local rivals Birmingham City 5-1, their biggest win in a Second City derby league fixture since the 1960s.

Ashley Young gave Villa the lead after 28 minutes and three minutes before halftime he took the free kick from which John Carew headed the second.

Eight minutes after the restart Carew tapped in a Gareth Barry pass to make it 3-0. Soon after the hour mark Young beat two players before firing in a low drive which was saved but only straight back into his path to score the rebound. Mikael Forssell pulled one back for the Blues but Gabby Agbonlahor got the fifth with twelve minutes to go, being let clean through after a defensive mistake.

Villa had been dominant in midfield and unstoppable up front, with Young outstanding in front of watching England manager Fabio Capello.

The win was Villa's biggest league win over the Blues since a 4-0 win in 1962-63. It kept them in the hunt for a European place with three games remaining and left their rivals in deep relegation trouble.

2010
FINALISTS IN THE
90 FIFTIETH LEAGUE CUP

Villa reached the final of the League Cup's fiftieth season, but despite taking an early lead were beaten by Manchester United.

Villa reached the final by beating Cardiff, Sunderland, Portsmouth and Blackburn. Manchester United, who Villa had defeated in the 1994 final, awaited them at Wembley.

In the fifth minute Gabriel Agbonlahor had his shirt pulled in the area leading to a penalty being awarded. James Milner converted the kick but seven minutes later United were level when Richard Dunne was dispossessed, leading to Michael Owen scoring.

Milner and United's Park Ji Sung both went close but the score remained level at the break. There were few chances in the second half then in the 74th minute Wayne Rooney's looping header gave United the lead.

Rooney almost extended United's lead soon afterwards but his header hit the post. In a frantic last ten minutes Emile Heskey's header ricocheted onto the crossbar and Dunne fired wide as United held on for victory.

Despite losing the final Villa still managed to qualify for Europe courtesy of a sixth place league finish.

Villa were plunged into a managerial crisis at the beginning of the 2010-11 season when Martin O'Neill resigned just five days before it was due to start.

During his four seasons in charge O'Neill had established Villa in the top half of the table and qualified for Europe on three occasions. He also took them to a first cup final in ten years.

On 9th August O'Neill stunned the club and fans by announcing his resignation with immediate effect. A statement on the club website thanked him for the past four years and said that there would be no further comment on the matter.

Two days later, chairman Randy Lerner said that the two did not have a common view on how to move the club forward. Speculation was rife that O'Neill was unhappy about the funds available for transfers, with no new signings having been made to far that summer.

Kevin MacDonald was placed in temporary charge of team affairs. Villa had a mixed start to the season, winning two and losing two of their opening five games before Gerard Houllier took over on 22nd September.

92

2011
A RECORD
SIGNING

The club's record transfer fee was the £24 million spent on striker Darren Bent in January 2011 but he failed to live up to expectations.

After he had submitted a transfer request to Sunderland, Villa splashed out the huge fee to bring Bent to the West Midlands on 18th January. He signed a four and a half year deal and four days later he scored a debut goal in a 1-0 win at home to Manchester City.

By the end of the season Bent scored nine goals in sixteen appearances, making him the club's joint top scorer alongside Ashley Young. The following season he was again top scorer with ten goals in a campaign that was ended in February by an ankle injury.

In 2012-13 the form of Christian Benteke and Gabby Agbonlahor saw Bent fall out of favour. He spent 2013-14 on loan at Fulham, for whom he scored three times as they were relegated from the Premiership.

The following season Bent played seven times for Villa without scoring before being sent on loan spells to Championship sides Brighton and Derby. In the summer of 2015 his contract came to an end and he joined Derby on a permanent deal.

After just nine months as manager, Gerard Houllier left Aston Villa in June 2011 after the recurrence of a previous heart problem.

Houllier, who had won three cups in one season with Liverpool and the French title twice with Lyon, was appointed in September 2010 after the resignation of Martin O'Neill.

Villa struggled in the first half of the season and weren't helped by injuries to key players. The arrival of new signings in the January transfer window saw an upturn in form and Villa climbed away from the relegation zone into twelfth place.

In March the team struggled again and a first home loss to Wolves in over thirty years led to sections of the crowd turning against Houllier. On 20th April he took ill and was admitted to hospital, leading to assistant Gary McAllister taking over for the rest of the season.

Villa lost only once in five games under McAllister and finished ninth. Despite hoping to return to the club, Houllier was told by doctors that this was inadvisable at the time due to his heart problems.

Given the medical advice and Villa's board feeling stability was required going into the new season, Houllier left the club by mutual consent.

2011
ASTON VILLA'S
OLDEST PLAYER

In 2010-11 Brad Friedel became Aston Villa's oldest ever player at the age of 39 years 259 days.

    The American international goalkeeper joined Villa for £2.5 million from Blackburn in 2008. He signed a three year deal and saved a penalty after just ten minutes of his debut in a friendly

at Reading. His league debut was a 4-2 home win over Manchester City, who had also expressed an interest in signing him.

    Friedel was a Premier League ever present in each of his the seasons at Villa. This was part of a sequence of 310 consecutive Premier League appearances spanning eight years and three clubs.

On 1st February Friedel became Villa's oldest ever player in game against Manchester United at Old Trafford. He had a busy afternoon, picking the ball out of the net in the first minute when Wayne Rooney scored. He went onto make a number of good saves but Villa went down 3-1.

Friedel continued to break the record for the rest of the season, his final appearance for Villa coming in a 1-0 home win over Liverpool on 22nd May, four days after his fortieth birthday. The following month he signed for Tottenham Hotspur.

FACT 95
ALEX MCLEISH REPLACED BY PAUL LAMBERT

After becoming the first manager to move directly from Birmingham City to Aston Villa, Alex McLeish lasted just one season before being replaced by Paul Lambert.

McLeish joined Villa on 17th June 2011 five days after resigning from the Blues, who he had just taken down to the Championship. He had a hard job to do in winning over Villa's fans, some of whom protested outside Villa Park and wrote graffiti at the training ground.

Villa struggled throughout the season and won just four home games, eventually finishing sixteenth and only two points above the relegation zone. The day after the season ended, McLeish was sacked and he was replaced at the beginning of June by another Scotsman, Paul Lambert.

Lambert came with good credentials. A European Cup winner as a player with Borussia Dortmund, he had guided Norwich from League One to the Premiership with back-to-back promotions. 2012-13 didn't turn out as hoped and Villa finished fifteenth, but there were signs of promise from youngsters and Lambert remained in charge for the following season.

After finishing fifteenth again in 2013-14 Lambert was again under scrutiny but he held on to his job. However in February 2015, with Villa in the relegation zone, he was sacked and replaced by Tim Sherwood.

Aston Villa's worst ever defeat came as recently as 23rd December 2012 when they were thrashed 8-0 by Chelsea at Stamford Bridge.

Villa had been in good form in preceding weeks and lost none of their last five league games. However they were 1-0 down after just two minutes when Fernando Torres scored. By halftime they trailed 3-0 thanks to a David Luiz free kick and Branislav Ivanovic header.

Frank Lampard made it 4-0 on the hour but it was in the last fifteen minutes that Villa completely fell apart, conceding four times. Ramires got the fifth and fellow substitute Oscar scored the sixth from the penalty spot. Eden Hazard then hit the seventh into the corner of the net.

Ciaran Clark then gave away a penalty but Brad Guzan saved Lucas Piazon's kick. It did become 8-0 in injury time however when Ramires got his second. Villa had been ripped apart by an outstanding Chelsea side inspired by Frank Lampard and they were lucky that the result hadn't gone into double figures.

It meant Villa had suffered their worst ever defeat. They had been beaten 7-0 on five previous occasions, the last being in 1964.

Former Aston Villa captain Stiliyan Petrov retired from playing in 2013 after a battle with cancer.

The Bulgarian followed manager Martin O'Neill from Celtic to Villa in August 2006, having spent seven years with the Scottish giants. His form was up and down in his first two seasons but a highlight was a volley from near the halfway line against Derby in April 2008.

Petrov's third season saw a vast improvement and he was a midfield regular in the side, ending the campaign with both supporters' player and players' player of the year accolades. He was then appointed captain for the following season.

After captaining Villa to the League Cup final and sixth place in the league, Petrov saw O'Neill resign but he kept the armband for the next two seasons, each of them under a different manager.

In March 2012 Petrov was diagnosed with leukaemia and he announced that he would be taking a complete break from football for treatment. Fans responded by applauding during the nineteenth minute of every game, his shirt number.

At the end of 2012-13 with the cancer in remission Petrov announced his retirement. He attended the final home game of the season against Chelsea and led his family on a lap of honour around the pitch.

Having been well beaten in the 2015 FA Cup final Villa didn't even have the consolation of a European place due to a new UEFA ruling.

Villa were drawn at home in every round, beating Blackpool, Bournemouth, Leicester and West Bromwich Albion. Villa were a different side under Tim Sherwood compared to Paul Lambert and in the semi-final they came from behind to beat Liverpool 2-1, booking a final date with holders Arsenal on 30th May.

The first half was mainly Arsenal with Shay Given making some important saves. Eventually Theo Walcott put the Gunners ahead six minutes before halftime. Villa rallied briefly after the break but a stunning goal from Arsenal's Alexis Sanchez in the fiftieth minute gave them a mountain to climb.

Shortly after the hour Per Mertesacker ended the game as a contest when he headed the third. Even the introduction of Gabby Agbonlahor failed to improve things. Villa's misery was completed in injury time when Olivier Giroud scored Arsenal's fourth goal.

In previous seasons the FA Cup runners up had been allowed into the Europa League if the winners had qualified for Europe via their league position. New UEFA rules however meant that this was no longer to be the case and what would have been Villa's place went instead to Southampton.

2016
99 THREE WINS, THREE MANAGERS & RELEGATED

2015-16 was a disastrous season for Aston Villa as they were relegated after 28 consecutive top-flight seasons. They won just three games all campaign, had three different managers and finished rock bottom of the table, 22 points from safety.

Villa started the season with Tim Sherwood in charge but after beating Bournemouth 1-0 on the opening day they lost eight of the next nine games, leading to his dismissal. He was replaced by Remi Garde but things didn't improve, with Villa not winning again until 12th January, the 21st game of the season.

A 2-0 win over Norwich on 6th February gave Villa a glimmer of hope. However the following week they were thrashed 6-0 at home by Liverpool, their worst defeat at Villa Park since 1935. This was the start of a club record eleven game losing sequence that meant relegation was confirmed with four matches still to go. By now Eric Black had been put in temporary charge for the rest of the season, Garde having left at the end of March.

Villa finished the season with a dismal seventeen points, the second worse total by any team ever in the Premiership. Villa had never managed such a low tally even before 1982 when only two points for a win were awarded.

The manager brought in to revive Aston Villa's fortunes after relegation was sacked after only just twelve games.

Villa turned to former West Bromwich Albion manager Roberto di Matteo, who had won the Champions League with Chelsea in 2012. He was appointed early in the close season and undertook a major overhaul of the squad, bringing in nine players and releasing or selling ten others.

After a positive pre-season Villa lost their opening game 1-0 at Sheffield Wednesday. They did beat Rotherham in their first home game but they failed to win any of their next eight fixtures. Villa were also dumped out of the League Cup by League Two Luton Town in the first round.

Di Matteo was sacked after a 2-0 defeat at Preston on 1st October that left the two places above the relegation zone. He was replaced by Steve Bruce, who had plenty of recent Championship experience with Hull City but had also managed Birmingham City for six years the previous decade.

Bruce's first game as a manager ended in 1-1 home draw with Wolves. However in his next match Villa won at Reading to record their first away win in over a year. The moved away from the danger zone with just two defeats in eleven games and eventually finished the season in thirteenth place.

The 100 Facts Series

Arsenal, *Steve Horton*	978-1-908724-09-0
Aston Villa, *Steve Horton*	978-1-908724-98-4
Celtic, *Steve Horton*	978-1-908724-10-6
Chelsea, *Kristian Downer*	978-1-908724-11-3
Everton, *Bob Sharp*	978-1-908724-12-0
Leeds, *Steve Horton*	978-1-908724-94-6
Liverpool, *Steve Horton*	978-1-908724-13-7
Manchester City, *Steve Horton*	978-1-908724-14-4
Manchester United, *Iain McCartney*	978-1-908724-15-1
Newcastle United, *Steve Horton*	978-1-908724-16-8
Norwich, *Steve Horton*	978-1-908724-99-1
Rangers, *David Clayton*	978-1-908724-17-5
Tottenham Hostpur, *Steve Horton*	978-1-908724-18-2
West Ham, *Steve Horton*	978-1-908724-80-9

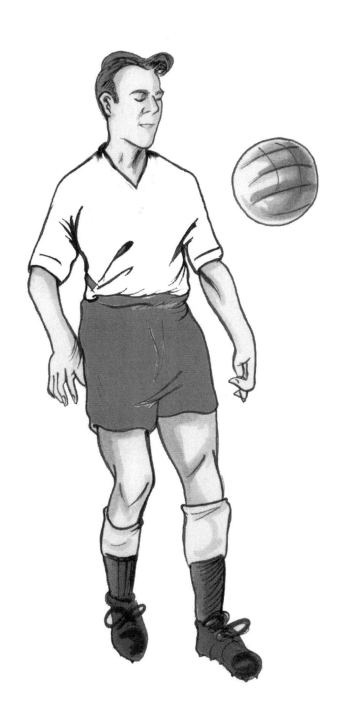